AF255499

DEDICATION

The Journey Within is dedicated to those who are determined to let their life's journey motivate them and inspire others. Life teaches us many things if we are quite enough to hear. Allow my experiences to awaken something in you that will give others hope. Happy reading!

ACKNOWLEDGMENTS

The Journey Within was borne out of a handful of inspirers who, without their continued support, would not have been written. I am eternally grateful for your steadfastness on this journey with me.

Maria Keener, Loretta Keener, Lauren Keener, Barrington McLean, Annie Anderson, Adassa Ellis, The Five AM Team.

TABLE OF CONTENTS

Chapter 1: Mango Walk A World Beyond the Hills.................................1

Chapter 2: Fruits, Fields, and Faith.................................5

Chapter 3: Steps of Faith and Curiosity 9

Chapter 4: Stepping into the Light.................................14

Chapter 5: A Journey Proposed.................................19

Chapter 6: Morning Visits and Quiet Reflections 23

Chapter 7: News About the Summer Trip.................................28

Chapter 8: A Sunday Walk and Inner Battles.................................33

Chapter 9: Talking With Daddy.................................40

Chapter 10: A Walk Around Town 45

Chapter 11: Visiting CC and Heading to the Farm.................................50

Chapter 12: Coffee Beans, Close Calls, and Mother's Strength.........55

Chapter 13: Mother's Lessons and Sunday Strolls 60

Chapter 14: Sunday Reflections and Community Life.................................65

Chapter 15: Journals, Memories, and Farewells.................................70

Chapter 16: Bible Study and Preparing for Departure.................................75

Chapter 17: Leaving Home With Faith and Fear 81

Chapter 18: Braids and Questions of Faith.................................86

Chapter 19: Closure Before Crossing Oceans.................................91

Chapter 20: My Last Goodbye and First Flight.................................96

Chapter 21: America A World Within a World.................................101

Chapter 22: An Arrangement I Could Not Refuse.................................106

Chapter 23: The Patio Conversation That Changed My Path 111

Chapter 24: My Troubled Heart 116

Chapter 25: Breaking Free Through Faith and Conviction 121

Chapter 26: God's Word Proved True After All 126

Chapter 27: Renewed Faith and a Promise to Serve................................130

Chapter 28: From Headship to His Lordship 135

Chapter 29: Learning to See Through His Eyes...139

Chapter 30: It Is Within Me 143

Chapter 31: Walking Away to Truly Walk with God 148

Chapter 32: Freedom Through the Will 152

Chapter 33: Liberation A Journey of Trust in Christ 156

Chapter 34: Learning to Love God Above All 160

Chapter 35: Discovering God Within Me 164

Chapter 36: Transformation Through Trials 169

Chapter 37: Resting in Sonship..174

CHAPTER 1: MANGO WALK A WORLD BEYOND THE HILLS

Mango Walk was the shortcut to the school in the district where I lived in the rural area of Kraal, Jamaica. The distance between the cottage-style house that I shared with five siblings and the only all-age school in the district seemed like a million miles away on foot. At the tender age of eight, walking to school was always an adventure, as I let my imagination "take" me to places I only dreamed of.

Mango Walk is infamously branded due to the mango trees that line the lengthy, narrow path that leads to the main road to the school. With its frightening precipice and extravagant rolling hills, it overlooked the Rio Minho River on one side, and the steep, rocky mountain on the other, partially covered with various vegetation and fruit trees that graced the mountainside. Walking to school was something that I looked forward to. During those moments, I allowed my thoughts, imagination, or curiosity to travel beyond the rolling mountains beneath the blue sky. I wondered what lay beyond the mountains. "Is there another world just behind the mountain peak?" I asked myself. "How can I get to that place that seems so far away?" I wondered.

On the way to school, I would stop and savor the exotic fruits that fell from the trees to the ground. The guavas were delicious, and the guineps were plump and sweeter than usual. The tambarines were a bit dry, but savory nonetheless. Mango season was fast approaching, and I could not wait for the Common and Kidney Mangoes to turn bright yellow/red or orange and fall from the humongous trees to be eaten. "God, will you please let the mangoes come quickly this year?" I asked. As a third grader, I did not understand who God was. Mother made sure that even if she did not go to church, my siblings and I went. The faint memory that I had of who God was when the preacher said that if we did something bad, God would not be pleased with us. I did not want God to not like me, so from that day forward, I had a keen awareness of being afraid to mess up.

Third grade, or grade three, was a big girl's grade, I recalled. I either had friends or I did not. At the end of the first week at the beginning of the school year, all the children either found their best friends or did not. My best friend was Cheryl. We did almost everything together. We sat next to each other in an inclusive classroom setting. We liked the same subjects and even the same snacks: homemade donkey corns and bag juices. Cheryl was quiet, but bossy, and I did not like to be bossed around. One day, Cheryl tried taking my hand-held pencil sharpener, and I told her that she could not have it. She snatched it from me, so I snatched it back, and the open blade left a scar on my hand. Cheryl and I were no longer friends. That experience left me wondering why our friendship had to end. "Maybe if I had allowed Cheryl to keep the pencil sharpener, we would have remained friends?" I asked myself. Guess I'll never know.

School had ended for the day, and it was time to walk home. The hot, tropical weather was pretty steamy that day as I walked up the steep hill from the school to the entry point of Mango Walk. The 20-minute walk home through Mango Walk was more tolerable because of the shade from the forestry scenic view. I stopped to look at the river at the foot of the hill while I allowed my curiosity to build on itself. I was curious about the stillness of the crisp, clean water flowing as if to no end. It made a sound that created an inner peace that I did not want to end. It was as though the river was conversing with itself as it danced with rhythmic buoyancy and pride. The rows of bladed grass, ferns, and daffodils graced the banks of the river with such beauty that it captivated my attention. The farm animals lined the banks of the river while they quenched their thirst from the scorching heat of the sun. Meanwhile, the tropical birds hovered over the glistening river while seemingly speaking to each other in an exotic language that only a genius could create.

It seemed that I had been sitting on the side of the mountain for hours, and I began wondering if my mother was looking for me, but I still could not stop my mind from wandering about the things that I had been observing for about 30 minutes, which seemed like hours. Curiosity became normal, it appeared. I had so many questions. Questions about the flowers, birds, river, trees, fruits…the list was endless. I got up and began walking home when I noticed my mother in the distance. I ran to her, and she picked me up and hugged me warmly. I suppose she was just as happy to see me as I was to see her.

As we continued home, I began asking her lots of questions.

"Why are there so many different kinds of trees?" "Where does the river begin, and where does it end?" Why are there so many different kinds of birds?" "Why do so many different kinds of flowers grow so close to the river?" I asked my mother. She found a flat stone alongside the road. She sat on it and held me on her lap.

Then she said, "I do not have the answers to your questions. All I can say is that God created them for us. Flowers are made to beautify the earth. Rivers are created for many reasons, but especially for cooking and washing. The fruit trees are made for food for people and animals," explained my mother. My mother was a very wordy person. She had a way of responding to questions with a bit of humor and lengthy answers. "Yes, mommy" I said in my Jamaican accent.

After a year or so, I moved away from Kraal to live with my father. He did not live too far away, so he and I occasionally visited the family farm, which was about 3 miles from the district. The farm was an inherited property from my father's grandfather. Though the journey across the Rhio Minor River to the top of the hill to the farm was sometimes treacherous, the incredible display of exotic fruits and vegetation made it worthy after all. The father-daughter chats were incredible. Needless to say, memories were created and cherished. Daddy (he was affectionately called) was quite soft-spoken and well learned. His memory seemed to be intact as he embellished our ancestral history.

He went on to say that his father's ancestors were from Africa, while his mother's were from Germany. His father was from the northeast side of the island, and shortly after my dad's birth, his father migrated to another country, so he did not know much about him. It was typical for many islanders to seek better job opportunities in other countries. Some would return and help their families, while others never returned. My dad never recalled seeing his father after he migrated to the United States of America. All he'd heard was that he was practicing medicine as a medical doctor somewhere in New York. Daddy never bothered to fact-check, I suppose.

CHAPTER 2: FRUITS, FIELDS, AND FAITH

While on the family farm, my dad took me to the plot of land that his grandfather willed to him.

The land was enriched with the most exotic fruit trees and vegetation as far as the eye could see. It was laced with coffee, cocoa, coconut, ackee, mango, banana, pimento, nutmeg, oranges, guineps, and plantain trees. Additionally, yams, cassava, pumpkin, gungu, and strawberries were just about ready to be harvested. Time would not allow me to mention other fruits and vegetables, such as avocado, apples, and soursop that God, according to my mother, "created for us to enjoy." The rolling hills overlooking the river below were a breathtaking view that had my curious heart asking questions that only my thoughts could hear. Daddy, unaware of my thoughts, continued reliving his memories of the family land while I stayed closely engaged with him.

"My grandfather, who was a farmer, was willed this piece of land by his father," said Daddy. "His parents were originally from Germany. They migrated to Jamaica during the time of exploration. They secured this property of over 20 acres all the way down to the river. My mother was born in that little structure," Daddy continued, "and so was I." The structure that Daddy was referring to was a 2-room frame that appeared to have endured the harshest of weather, yet remained standing. The floor was made of cement, board and partially dried mud. The mud was designed to store the rain boots, or water boots, when my great-grandfather came from harvesting food for supper. The frame was made of blocks, and the roof was of zinc. The kitchen and bathroom were independent of the main structure. (That was the custom of that era). "My grandfather and I would go to the field together sometimes, where he taught me how to farm," Daddy continued. "All of these fruits and vegetables that you are seeing were planted by him. Below the hill, there are lots more to see. He also had animals. Donkeys, cows, goats, chickens, and hogs. The chickens or fowls laid eggs. The common fowls were the layers, and the white ones were for dinner. It was important to know the difference," said Daddy. The donkeys were used to transport food and water, while the cows produced milk and meat for the family. The hogs produced piglets. The family sold them to support the farm along with the goats," continued Daddy. I looked forward to those teachable moments.

Daddy and I continued exploring the land and its contents. Mosquitoes were everywhere, and they were not afraid to attack relentlessly. Daddy had a remedy for them, and that was a homemade torch that was made of a regular-sized soda bottle, kerosene, and newspaper. He used the match to light the engulfed newspaper, and the mosquitoes disappeared.

"Whew," I said in relief. As we trod down to the other side of the property, I noticed rows of orange trees that were neatly organized. Daddy explained that the oranges, along with the other farm fruits and vegetation, were taken by the donkeys to the market for sale. He recalled those days as laborious. The soil was difficult to cultivate sometimes, he explained, and digging cassava, potatoes, and yams from the soil was extremely difficult for a young boy. There was no heavy machinery to assist, so a butcher's knife, a cutlass, or a machete were the main tools to use. Every swing or cut of those tools took energy, and the scorching tropical sun did not make life easier. After gathering all of the fruits and vegetables and loading them into the donkey's hampers, it was time to tread the long, narrow paths across the shallow parts of the river bed to the other side of the town to the market vendor's stands. That was where goods and services were exchanged in the open market. Daddy recalled that since he was the only child of his mother, he was the only one to tread the journey every Saturday to the market. Maybe such an experience propelled him to join the police force, where he ultimately became a police officer. Daddy never gave up his love for the farm, and he continued visiting when his job would allow breaks.

Dusk was upon us, so it was time to head home. The experience on the farm was memorable, but it left me questioning "life." "What is this life really about?" I asked myself back then and now. "Why did daddy, an only child, endure such hardship at such a young age, even missing going to school numerous times to help out on the farm?" I questioned myself.

My siblings and I were in daddy's care after our mother migrated to another country for better opportunities for her family. (Migration to other countries was the norm for many household members who wanted better economic opportunities for themselves and their family members).

I was 11 years old when Daddy took me to live with my cousin in the town of Four Paths. Four Paths is about 10 miles from Kraal. I attended the district's all-aged school in the fifth grade. The teachers were very nice and strict. The students were mannerly and focused on their school work, and they dared not get off task because the learning environment did not allow that. I became friendly with quite a few students, but there was one dear classmate with whom I was inseparable. We have been friends for over 40 years. After living with my cousin for about a year, Daddy reunited my older sister and me and moved us to another community not too far from Four Paths. My sister had been living with a family friend after my mother migrated.

I was around 12 years old when daddy relocated because of his job. He took my older sister and me with him while our brothers lived with other relatives. My sister and I were inseparable. She and I were placed with a family that our father knew very well in a community known as Bird's Island, about 3 miles from Kraal. We stayed with that family for about 3 - 4 years. I had some great memories in that community that will stay with me forever. After my sister turned 18, she embarked on her adult life, so I was now solo. I missed my sister dearly because she was a very nice person, not only to me, but those who knew her.

Daddy's line of work in law enforcement placed him in various districts on the southeast side of the island. I was also relocated to different Boarding Homes to be closer to him. Those homes were designed to include atmospheres that were conducive to my education, as daddy was a father who fostered education.

The first Boarding Home was located in the Blackwoods district. Blackwoods was about 15 miles from where Daddy was stationed. I was about 16 years old. The family that I boarded with was very nice. The couple owned a small grocery store that served the community of about 1,000 residents. They were God-fearing, so I was encouraged to go to church every Sunday, which I did because I was curious about the things of the Bible. Though I read the Bible, especially the Old Testament, the only takeaway was the fear of going to hell. I remembered very vividly the nightmares that I would have about hell, so I became very afraid to do anything that would cause me to end up there. Needless to say, there was a whole lot more to the Bible than the parts about hell. I was left more confused after reading the Bible than when I started. It all seemed to contradict itself, so I became very curious about finding out what it really was about.

CHAPTER 3: STEPS OF FAITH AND CURIOSITY

The Bible, or the Great Book as I like to refer to it, is fascinating to me. It's intriguing because it seems to contradict itself; yet, it appears to be a blueprint, guide, or manual to help mankind function on this planet, Earth.

My earliest memory of the Bible was around age 5. Mother would send my siblings and me to the only church in the Kraal district. I went there for Sunday services. On a particular Sunday, I do not recall what the sermon was about, but I had the most frightening dream that Sunday night. My house was located not too far from the entrance of Mango Walk. In the dream, I was standing about 15 feet away from the main road. A huge circular black hole appeared in front of me. On top of the massive black hole was written in red, David.

Over 45 years have passed, and I can still envision the dream. Amazing. I still do not have any idea what the dream means, but one thing is for sure, until this day, there is such a reverential awe of the Creator of this vast world and its content that I cannot begin to articulate. Because of that experience, I have consciously set out to find out about the God and Jesus of the Bible. The quest and curiosity continue. All I know is that, throughout the short life I have lived so far, my human capabilities continue to be challenged and stretched in ways that convince me there is a superpower, being, God, Spirit... at work, one that the Bible cannot truly define, respectfully.

After a year, Daddy decided that it was time for me to leave Blackwoods and relocate to Crooked River to live with my aunt. I was 17 years old. Crooked River is located about 20 miles from Blackwoods. Daddy was stationed not too far from Crooked River.

While living with my aunt, I continued attending church, burning with the same passion to discover who the God of the Bible was. After about 6 months of living with my aunt, she became ill, so I was relocated to another Boarding House in the community or town that was located in the city of Chapelton, known as Sangster's Heights. One of the first things I did after relocating to the Sangster's Heights community was search for a church to attend.

Finding a church to call home was very important to me. By that point, I was learning about water baptism. I had learned that water baptism was a significant step in the Christian faith. I did not know much about it, but I wanted to do whatever I needed to be "right" with God.

Daddy was stationed within walking distance of Sangster's Heights. He and I had a very close bond, so much so that my mother's phrase for me was "You are your daddy's pocket book." Oh Lord. I also recalled her saying that in her day, it was common for at-home births. Daddy, she told me, was the one who read the medical book and gave instructions to the midwife... a dear friend of the family...about the delivery process, including where to cut my umbilical cord. Daddy's name, mother continued, is Earl Winston Marshall. He named me Winsome Marshall. The name Winsome, I recalled her saying, was symbolic of daddy's first name, Winston. After hearing that story, I spent the rest of my life trying to do everything Daddy asked of me. I wanted to make him proud. Shortly after graduating from high school, Daddy enrolled me at the local college. It was within walking distance to his job and also where I resided.

The college was located about 3 miles from where I resided. On Wednesdays, I stopped by the station on my way to college to visit Daddy. I looked forward to those visits. He was a police constable, so he spent quite a bit of time in the compound and wrote in a large, thick ledger that was on the main counter of the office. Police work.

I spent time watching him write. He seemed to enjoy what he did. Daddy would allow me to accompany him while he visited the prisoners. There were always just a handful of them. They looked forward to seeing him. As soon as they saw him, they would shout, "Mr. Marshall. Wha gwaan?" Wha gwaan (Patois) means how are you?

Those who knew Mr. Marshall seemed to take a strong liking to him, I recalled. To them, he was not just a typical police officer. Mr. Marshall, as he was professionally known, was a kind man, people would say to me. He was very soft-spoken, and he truly valued each person regardless of their status in life. The prisoners seemed to embrace that truth as well. I was proud to be in Daddy's presence because he cared about people. I, too, was quite amazed at the level of compassion Daddy had towards people. I recalled my mother saying that Daddy was a Sunday school teacher at his family's church when he and my mother met. His mild demeanor, tolerance, and compassion for the less fortunate were incredible to see demonstrated, especially in his line of duty. I often wondered if Daddy's experience with the church environment contributed to his care towards others, and why he was so different from so many who also attended church and took part in church activities.

My Wednesday visit with Daddy had ended, and I was off to college. On the way there and back, I reminisced about the prisoner's behaviour towards my father. I did not know why their behaviour affected me that much, but when I got home that afternoon, I decided to attend the Wednesday night church service at the holiness church that I began attending when I moved to the Sangster's Heights community. The church was about 0.5 miles from where I lived. Before I left home to visit the night's service, I recalled having a conversation with the owner of the boarding house where I was residing. She was a most esteemed Jamaican-born lady who had spent most of her adult life residing and working in the UK. She had retired from there, built her dream home in Jamaica, and was now living a most comfortable life. A Boarder or the owner of boarding homes typically housed students whose parents were economically stable, because boarding homes were costly. As stated before, Daddy embraced the field of education, and he did not mind investing in my educational journey. One of Daddy's expectations was that I not leave the premises without telling the owner of my whereabouts. "Ms. Manning and I must know your whereabouts," Daddy said to me in a most calm but direct tone. Obedience was nonnegotiable with most Jamaican parents, so that was a no-brainer.

Ms. Manning was an Anglican Church member. That view catered to the higher classes. Upon hearing that I was off to the holiness church around the block, Ms. Manning calmly said with a heavy British accent, "Off you go, my dear. Enjoy!" She had a most positive outlook on life, and she did so with the most striking smile and confidence that were contagious. Of all the landlords that I had boarded with, Ms. Manning was the most enthusiastic of all, who lived her life with much gratitude and appreciation. She was generous and kind to all that she came in contact with. She was very dedicated to her church family and often gave God credit openly.

After bidding Ms. Manning farewell, I was off to the holiness church.

At age 17, I was curious about so many things. Daddy had already warned me about boyfriends and encouraged me to stay away from dating until after graduation. I had not had a chance to make friends in the new environment, so I walked to church, solo. The 0.5-mile-long walk seemed like forever. There was only one street light between the boarding home and the church. It was about 7:00 pm, and the main street to the church was dark. There were quite a few homes and businesses on the path to the church, and most of them had light poles in front of their properties, but for some odd reason, no light was displayed from them. I had hoped otherwise, since I was new to the area and didn't know much about the community. I was now about 7 minutes away from the church. There was a dark bend on the street to go around to get to the other side of the road. I was very afraid. I travelled on the same road almost daily to get back and forth to school, the grocery store, or to get to town, but never after dark. Wednesday night service began at 7:00 pm. My watch showed 7:05 pm, so all the early attendees had gone ahead. I was alone. I could hear dogs barking from their backyards, which meant that they were watching the owners' yards for intruders. The fear of the darkness gripped me so terribly that I almost turned around and went back home. I had a dilemma.

CHAPTER 4: STEPPING INTO THE LIGHT

My older sister, with whom I lived for a bit, attended church quite often. I recalled her praying every night before she went to sleep. I did not know how to pray, really, because I did not understand how prayer worked. Here I was in a dilemma, and I was determined to go to church, so I mustered up the courage to pray to the God that my sister prayed to and of whom the preacher at the Kraal community church preached about. "If you are real, God, let me walk through this darkness and be alright," I said in my heart. I closed my eyes and walked with trembling legs and sweaty palms. When I opened my eyes, I was on the other side of the road in a lit area. I still recall that moment. That moment of answered prayer may seem trivial, but it was significant to my trust in the God of the Bible. In no time, I was at the church. The members were singing and playing all kinds of instruments. I joined in with them. During the altar call, the young minister beckoned for anyone who needed prayer to go to the altar to be prayed over. I went. When it was my turn to be prayed for, the preacher asked, "Winsome, what is your prayer request tonight?" "I would like to be saved," I responded.

I did not understand what save meant. It was the usual term that I had heard others say during an altar call, but all I knew was that God helped me through the darkness on my way to church, and I wanted to show Him that I was thankful, so I wanted to be saved. The preacher laid his hand on my head and prayed for me to be saved.

Six months had passed since I had gotten saved. The women of the church took me through the proper procedures to become a member. My Christian (first name) and Surname (last name) were placed in the church registry. Next, I was openly asked by the preacher, pulpit, and the congregation if I agreed to become a member of the church. Then, I was given an outline of scriptures, dates, and duties to solidify my membership. After completing the protocols, I was an official member. Next was water baptism.

Mother had returned from her international trip. My baptism was coming up, and I wanted her to attend. She agreed. We had an opportunity to talk before I got baptized. "Winsome, I think that you are too young to be baptized," said Mother. "You are only 17 years old," she continued.

Mother had a point. My life consisted of two important things, according to Daddy. They were (1) finished school and graduate, (2) had no boyfriends. Pretty straightforward, I would say. "Mommy, I know that I am only 17 years old, but I do not have much going on. I can be baptized and still do what Daddy asked of me." I responded to my mother. "Alright. Do what you think is best," said my mother. The big day had arrived. It was baptism day. The baptism line was white and long. Women and teenage girls dressed in all white dresses as a sign of purity. Inside the baptism pool stood the pastor and a deacon, dressed in black clothing as they prepared to perform the baptisms.

The Sunday evening sky was overcast and seemed to lend its blessing on such an occasion. I could see my mother standing on the sidelines watching the action with a firm look on her face as though she was hoping that I'd changed my mind. Daddy had to work the evening shift, but I doubted if he would have attended such an occasion, as he was not involved much in church since he had joined the police force.

As I stood in the baptism line, mixed emotions flooded my mind. Emotions of doubts, fears, anxiousness, excitement, and questions. I knew nothing about this newly found life's transition that I was about to embark on, but I had an intuition that I should. One thing that I was convinced of was that I did not want to go to hell, and I did not want to do anything to cause God to punish me. The pastor's message in Kraal resonated with me, I supposed.

There were two women ahead of me in the baptism line. One of them appeared to be well prepared, while the other seemed uneasy. The first one was beckoned by the two men in the water to step down inside the pool. After 5 minutes, the other one did the same. It was my turn. I glanced at my mother, who had the same doubtful look in her eyes. Nevertheless, I took the first step towards the pool and waited to be called inside the water. My heart was racing with excitement and fear simultaneously. I was determined to press on anyway. "Sister Winsome, you may step down into the water," said the pastor. He and the deacon reached out their hands and grabbed hold of mine as I stepped into the water. It had only been less than one minute when I was asked to repeat the typical baptism rituals, but it seemed like an hour had passed as the thoughts ran through my mind. A moment of doubt captured my thoughts, and I began to rethink going through with such a major move. "Is mother correct?" I thought. "Am I getting baptized too young?" I asked myself.

The stories that I had heard about the Christian life were that Christianity was boring. I would not be able to date, go to parties, listen to worldly music, drink alcohol, or the like. As far as I was concerned, I had no interest in those few "sins" anyway, so I was not missing out on anything. Plus, finishing school would have kept me busy enough that I would not even have time to indulge those activities. "Repeat after me, Sister Winsome." Said the pastor. It was as though I was daydreaming and brought to reality. I repeated the formal baptismal oath. Next, I was immersed in the water and brought up a new creation, I was told by the preacher. It was official. My new life had begun.

I spent the next two years finishing up school and diligently participating in every church function that I was asked to attend. School attendance was something that I looked forward to. Making high passing grades and maintaining self-discipline were expected by my father. Pleasing him was foremost; therefore, academic success was accomplished with great joy. I liked seeing the joy on my father's face each time he heard of some sort of educational accomplishment. He had heard of my baptism, but did not say much about it. There was a knowing within me, if you will, that nothing should hinder my education. Additionally, Daddy was paying for boarding school, so I did not want to let him down. A few months after my birthday, Daddy came to me with a proposal.

Daddy wanted me to take a trip to America. The college that I was attending implemented a practice to award the graduating classes an opportunity to travel internationally at the end of the school year. It was a way of rewarding the students for their hard work and accomplishments. It was apparent that Daddy thought it was a great idea because he informed me ahead of time that he had wanted to discuss something with me during one of my Wednesday visits with him at the station. He rarely set up meetings or appointments with me, so I was curious about what he wanted to talk about. It must be important, I conversed within myself. He had arranged for us to meet the following day at a bookstore within walking distance from his workplace. On the way home, the "what ifs" bombarded my mind. What if I have to move again? What if Daddy's job post was relocating? What if there was something about his health? I could not wait for the next day to meet with him. It was almost the beginning of summer. Excitement filled the air. I had so many things that I wanted to do during the summer, I could not contain myself. That evening, I stayed up late chatting with Ms. Manning, the landlord. She had wanted us to visit Great Britain during the summer for the past two summers. Daddy did not think that it was a good idea then. He wanted me to settle in properly first. Ms. Manning went on and on about the monuments, parks, London

Bridge, clothing stores, cafes, and the like that England consisted of. I was excited! She painted such a beautiful picture of that strange land that I swore that I was there! She asked me what I thought about her suggestions. At the prime age of 19, who would not want to go to such an exciting place, I thought to myself. Of course, I said yes! She went on to say that she would have a conversation with my father and that she hoped that he would be on board.

CHAPTER 5: A JOURNEY PROPOSED

Thursday had arrived. It was time for my father and me to meet up for a discussion. The meeting was set for the afternoon, around 4:00 pm. I was to meet him at the station so that we could both go to the bookstore together. The walk from my home to the station was a bit melancholy; yet, promising somehow. The excitement came from a possible trip to Great Britain, I supposed? I could not tell. The sun was not as hot, strangely, compared to the dreaded heat that Jamaica normally produced between May and August. As a new convert, I began questioning the God of the Bible. The 15-minute walk gave me the opportunity to do so. I was unexplainably peaceful in my thoughts or spirit. I could not tell the difference. All of a sudden, trees, brightness of the sun, sounds of tropical birds, people, landforms, livestock, just about everything seemed to take on a different look. Or was it me who was seeing them differently, I reasoned with my own thoughts. That trend seemed to be the norm as of late. The God of the Bible was a stranger to me. Since the age of about 5 years old, I had developed a most passionate awareness of Him, strangely. That huge black hole with the name David written in red had captured my thoughts. I had developed some kind of passion to seek out something or someone amazing. Someone who created those fruit trees that I saw on Mango Walk. I heard so many stories about Him that were very interesting. Almost unbelievable to be frank. I recalled the first book that I read at that tender age. It was called My Book of Bible Stories.

In the small community of Kraal, my mother allowed me to visit our cousin, Ms. Daughter. I still do not know (nor did I ever think about asking) her proper name. Ms. Daughter resided only a few yards from my mother's house. Often, my mother allowed me to visit Ms. Daughter and kept her company since she was advanced in age and almost bedridden. She loved to read, but was unable to due to her partial sight. She was excited to see me because she would ask me to read for her. She enjoyed Bible tales. I still do not remember whose book it was, but I was given My Book of Bible Stories to read. I still recall the color, design, and writing of that book. I like beautiful manuscripts, and the way that the red title was written on that brass-gold-looking hardcover book was fascinating. I recalled reading about Noah and how he did what God wanted him to do. I liked the pictures and script of the book as well. That book created an eagerness to know more about God. I had reached the top of the hill and was within walking distance of the station. I could see Daddy walking towards the exit to meet me.

Daddy was not a hugger and neither was I. It was a cultural thing, I supposed. We greeted each other in a most respectful and gentle way. We were off to the bookstore. On the way there, Daddy asked if I was hungry. "Yes," I responded. There were several eateries in the town of Chapelton, the town where Daddy was stationed. Jamaica is known for producing the best beef patties. We both decided on patties for a snack, and so we grabbed a couple along with two Tings or grapefruit flavored drinks. We did not have enough time to sit and eat at the restaurant, so we ate and chatted a bit as we walked to the bookstore. Daddy asked about my day, and I did likewise. I asked him about the prisoners that I had met not too long ago. I wanted to know how they were doing. He told me that they had served their time and had gone home. I was relieved. I had a deep feeling that somehow, Daddy had made a positive impact on them and that they would fare better as free men. Those were my hopeful thoughts, anyhow. We arrived at the bookstore. It was almost empty because the students who normally flocked there were either preparing for summer or taking exams. Mr. Green, the bookstore owner, and his wife were acquaintances with Daddy. They all greeted each other with a most genuine greeting that seemed to be embedded in respect and fondness. Daddy had worked in that area for a number of years. He was known as the nicest police officer in that region. He was well-known and well-received by almost everyone. It made me feel good to be his daughter. After daddy greeted the Greens, he beckoned for me to have a seat in a less-trafficked area of the store at a small table with two chairs. After we were both seated, he clasped his hands together, placed them on the table in front of him, and began the conversation.

I had never seen my father with such a sullen look on his face. The look in his eyes seemed far away. I waited expectantly for what he wanted to talk about. "Do you remember me mentioning something to you about a trip that Clarendon College (CC) is planning for its graduates to the US?" he asked. "Yes, daddy," I said. It was typical for a Jamaican child, whatever the age, to address their mother as mummy or mommy and their father as daddy. "I am considering you going as well. What do you think?" he asked. I was surprised that Daddy asked my permission about the trip because it was understood in the Jamaican culture that parents who provided for any of their stay-at-home children do not ask their permission about hardly anything. There was an expectation that the parents would make all the decisions. "I do not know, Daddy. If you think that's what I should do, then that is what I will do." I responded to him.

The truth was, I wanted to visit England with Ms. Manning for the summer break, or Canada. I had lots of close family members in both countries. I knew of no close relatives in America except daddy's father, who supposedly had migrated there and became a doctor. There were a handful of family members who lived in Florida, but I was not close to them. "I have a good friend who lives in America. He is like a brother to me. I would like to send you to him to see what America is like," said Daddy. "You have completed your studies as I have asked you to do. Now, I want you to go and experience somewhere different," continued Daddy. "Alright, Daddy, I will go," I said. "Winsome, this trip will be different. When you go, my friend will tell you what to do. I will give you more information over the next two months before you leave for America," said Daddy. It was almost 6:00 pm. Daddy had to work the night shift, and I was returning home. We said goodbye to each other and parted ways.

The walk back home seemed surreal. I began mulling over the conversation that Daddy and I had. I also wondered how I was going to break the news to Ms. Manning, my landlord. She and I were looking forward to visiting Great Britain. I also wondered about my conversion. Thoughts flooded my mind. I had a passion for helping those who had medical issues, so I wanted to pursue nursing. During college, I frequented the local hospital just to get an up-close visual of what the site looked like. I had no clearance to enter private rooms and conversed with the patients, but I wanted to nonetheless. I did not tell my father about my aspirations because I did not want to thwart his plans for me. I trusted him probably more than I should have at the mature age of 19 years old.

CHAPTER 6: MORNING VISITS AND QUIET REFLECTIONS

I opened the front gate to the yard. Ms. Manning was sitting on the veranda while she casually looked at the passersby on the main road that went past the front of the house. Her smile was contagious. "Hello, Winsome. How did the conversation go with your father?" She asked in her broad British accent. Earlier that evening, I had told her that I was going to town to meet with Daddy because he wanted to talk with me. "Interesting," I responded. "It was very interesting, Ms. Manning," I repeated. I wanted to tell her that I would not be visiting Great Britain with her for the summer, but I did not want to disappoint her. She had been talking about it over the past year, and was looking forward to Daddy allowing me to travel with her. She had grown fond of me shortly after I began boarding with her. We would have lengthy conversations about her life, including her children's. She told me that I reminded her of one of her daughters, whom she was close to. It made sense to me then. She had grown attached to me and treated me as her own. Daddy's goal for me was to keep me focused on my education, so he paid the landlords to ensure that all domestic responsibilities were taken care of so that I could stay focused on my school work. Ms. Manning complied so much that she hired two helpers to suit my father. I was surprised that she took such an interest because one helper had been sufficient with the previous landlords. My rationale was that her daughter must have been special to her before leaving Jamaica to reside in Great Britain. Or, was it because Ms. Manning's mother's last moments were witnessed by me, and I called for help?

Ms. Manning was very close to her mother. Her mother was living with her when I arrived. After a while, the mother became ill and suffered a stroke. Ms. Manning had gone to run some errands, so I volunteered to keep an eye on her mother while she was away.

Shortly after she left to go to town, the mother suffered a stroke. I summoned Nurse Anderson, who lived next door to us. She came over to the house and noticed the mother's condition. She called the ambulance and had her taken to the hospital. Ms. Manning became aware of the situation and was pleased with how her mother's condition was attended to. She began addressing me as Nurse Marshall. Whatever the reason was, Ms. Manning was more than kind to me, and I was thankful. Our conversation ended over dinner, and I retired to my room.

It was 9:00 PM. I showered, brushed my teeth, and got in bed. As I lay, the day's activities replayed in my mind. The conversation with Daddy was surreal. In my 19-year-old mind, I could not fathom why I was going to be meeting up with my dad's best friend and what it was that he would share with me. In the Jamaican culture, it was not customary for parents to engage in detailed conversations with their children, so I knew not to ask Daddy for any details. I sure wanted to. I was a curious person (still am) who had a keen interest in my surroundings. On many occasions, I attempted to ask my parents questions that I wanted answers to, but the opportunity never presented itself where I felt comfortable enough. This moment was one of them. Oh, how I wanted to know more. I wanted to know what my father was thinking. One thing I knew was that it was not because of hardship or economic issues that Daddy was sending me off to his best friend. Daddy was blessed by his grandfather, where I could have gone to any university in Jamaica, and Daddy could have secured a well-to-do job for me because of his many connections. I ruled out hardship, so "Why was daddy sending me away?" I asked myself out loud. During the conversation, Daddy told me who the person was that he was sending me to. He was from the Kraal district. Daddy went on to say that they both met during a casual outing when they were young men. They remained friends throughout their adulthood. I knew the family very well. They were close to our family as well, and we all had a courteous relationship. I felt at ease after Daddy revealed that much to me. The following day was a Thursday. It was the beginning of June and the first day of summer break from school.

I slept in and rested most of the day. Ms. Manning had gone to run some errands, so I was home with the housekeeper. She and I had a good relationship. When I was not studying or ironing my school uniforms, she and I would chat while she worked. Our conversations were mostly silly but interesting. I shared with her that I was getting ready to leave the island for a visit to America. She was excited. She wanted to know where exactly I was going and for how long. If I were returning after the break ended or stayed longer. I had no solid answers for her, and she was obviously disappointed. I understood. We decided to change the conversation and talked about something that was not bittersweet. Cherry (that was her name) liked baking fruit cakes. We spent the remainder of the afternoon prepping and baking one of the best-tasting fruit cakes that I had eaten. Ms. Cherry and I had lots of fun times together. Unfortunately, she had to relocate to another part of the island due to unforeseen circumstances. I missed her. Ms. Manning hired another housekeeper. She was much younger than Ms. Cherry. She was very militant and did not take time to socialize. I did not want to interrupt her focus, so I stayed out of her way. She would smile at me, but seemed to be afraid to take time to socialize. I concluded that her last employer must have made her feel terrible, because she did not want to mix business with pleasure. Guess I will never know.

It was mid-afternoon. Ms. Manning had returned from running errands. "Winsome. I saw your father while I was out. He told me to tell you that he was coming by tomorrow afternoon after work. He wants to talk with you and me about something," said Ms. Manning. "Oh, alright," I responded. I had an idea of what Daddy wanted to discuss. It was apparent that he had not spoken to Ms. Manning about the trip. I did not want to be the one to break the news to her, so I was relieved that Daddy planned to have a conversation about it.

Friday arrived. I did my usual around-the-house stuff and was prepared for the discussion in the afternoon. Ms. Manning had asked the housekeeper to freshen up the house a bit and to prepare Snapper fish for dinner. Daddy loved steamed fish, especially Snappers. I prepared one of the household's favorite punches made of guavas, passion fruits, oranges, condensed milk, nutmeg, and dragon stout drink.

The residence was quite unique. Nestled at the intersection of two adjoining roads, the 3-bedroom, 2-bath, 1,700 sq ft home was a beauty to behold. It was custom-designed with a spacious living room, laundry, spacious kitchen, burglar-barred veranda, and an enclosed carport. The backyard was decked with a padded green, luscious lawn that was the envy of the neighborhood. Ms. Manning took pride in having the home decorated with a mixture of island/English-style decor that was quite appealing and attractive. Daddy was a simple fellow. Though he appreciated comfort, he preferred a simple living; however, he appreciated the efforts that were made to welcome him to dinner. Dinner was prepared and waiting on warmers. We heard the gate open and a light tap on the grill at the entrance of the veranda. It was Daddy. With a bright, welcoming smile, Ms. Manning exclaimed, "Hello, Mr. Marshall! It is so good to see you. Come in, will you?" Daddy wore a smile on his face, it seemed. There was never a moment that I saw him as unpleasant. "Yes, thank you," he replied. Customarily, greetings with hugs were unusual, so Daddy and I smiled at each other as a form of acknowledgement. He took off his police boots and placed them in a designated area of the tiled floor as the customs were. The housekeeper greeted him with a militant yet welcoming smile. She directed us to the decorative dinner table where the China dinner sets were arranged. After serving the lovely meal, the housekeeper excused herself to continue her duties, though she was offered to dine with us. It was to be expected.

After praying over the meal, Ms. Manning continued her greetings, then said, "Mr. Marshall, I must admit that after our conversation yesterday, I've been curious about what it is that you want to discuss," in a calm yet direct tone.

CHAPTER 7: NEWS ABOUT THE SUMMER TRIP

Daddy turned slightly toward Ms. Manning's direction and said, "I am aware that you and I agreed for Winsome to remain at your residence until the end of the year; however, I must change my plans," said Daddy. "As you are aware, Clarendon College is planning its yearly summer international trip to America, and I have decided to let Winsome go with her graduating class."

Upon hearing that, Ms. Manning appeared a bit stunned but excited. "Congratulations, Winsome! I am delighted to hear!" replied Ms. Manning in her deepest British tone. "When is she leaving and for how long, Mr. Marshall?" she asked.

"Next month. I am not sure of the date as yet, because I have some paperwork to file. I will let you know the exact date two weeks prior," Daddy responded.

The dinner gathering continued for another hour or so. Each of us expressed our gratitude and well-wishes towards each other as we all embarked on our individual life journeys. Before dinner ended, Ms. Manning beckoned that she wanted to meet with me before I retired to bed.

The next month was July, and it was fast approaching. There was a lot to do to prepare for the trip. Dinner ended, and Daddy went back to the station. It was around 7:00 PM. Ms. Manning asked me if she and I could chat for a bit in the living room. I said yes.

"Did you know about this international trip to America, Winsome?" She asked.

"Yes, I did, Ms. Manning," I replied.

"Why didn't you say something to me? I would've planned a

going-away-graduation party for you," she said.

"That is so kind of you, Ms. Manning, but I did not want to disappoint you. I knew that you were eager for you and me to visit Great Britain. I would still like to go, but I also did not want to disappoint my father," I said.

Ms. Manning looked at me with the kindest smile, lightly pinched my cheek, and said, "I am going to miss you dearly."

I watched her walk to her room and closed the large, heavy door behind her. I suspected that she was saddened by the news.

It was 8:00 PM. I took a shower, brushed my teeth, and retired to my room. I had practiced not going to sleep without praying, so I knelt by the bed and prayed. I did not know how to pray, so I repeated the customary prayer of the church.

In my heart, I felt like I needed to pray more or about something else, but I did not want to divert from the customs of the church's practices. I took the baptism very seriously and also all of the practices and traditions. I did not want to cross God nor the pastor and madams of the church.

The next day was Saturday. I had a cousin who lived up the road from my residence, so I decided to visit with her after breakfast. I was about 3 years older than she was, so she looked up to me, she confessed numerous times. She was born with a birth defect that affected one side of her body, so she walked with a limp.

She had the fairest, beautiful skin tone and long, flowing brown hair with slightly hazel and green eyes. Often, she would accompany me halfway up the road as I walked to school. Before I turned the corner, she stood and waved until we couldn't see each other anymore.

In those days, people with birth defects were shunned. I did not know why, but I comforted myself by saying that as long as my cousin knew that she was accepted, she would be okay.

When she saw me outside her gate, she ran towards me with a big smile. I took her hand, and we walked to the corner store, which was about 8 minutes away from her house. The corner store sold many of her favourite snacks, I discovered after taking a number of trips there over the past year.

On the way to and from the store, she and I talked about any and everything that we could. She seemed to enjoy my company as much as I enjoyed hers. She could not articulate what she wanted to say to me quite well due to a speech impediment, but somehow, I managed to get what she wanted to convey to me.

We were about two minutes away from her house when I told her that I wanted to talk to her about something. I felt a knot in my stomach before I revealed to her that I was getting ready to leave the island. I gathered that she would not take the news well.

Over the past year, I had not seen her socializing with anyone. There were a number of school-aged kids who resided in the community, but my cousin never managed to find any who remained friends with her. Telling her that the only person close to her age was getting ready to leave her as well was more than I could bear.

As I pondered over what to say, I began examining what a lie was. "Should I lie to her to protect her by not telling her that I was leaving, or should I tell her that I would be leaving the country, but I would be back very soon?" I questioned myself.

Lying was one of the three major sins according to preaching, so I had better not lie, especially after baptism. That was my justification anyway. I did not know when or if I would be back, so my thoughts were certainly going wild.

"What do you want to tell me, cuz?" she asked with a raspy, firm tone.

"Daddy wants me to take a little trip to America, but I should be returning soon, I think," I said to her.

Breaking the news to her in that fashion seemed befitting, so I did.

"Why are you going to America?" she asked.

She would not have grasped the reason why I was going cognitively, so I did not elaborate. Instead, I explained to her that I would be back after a while, and I promised to visit her.

She seemed relieved with the answer, but began tearing up. I comforted her and assured her that she was going to be alright. I escorted her home and closed the gate behind her.

We waved at each other until I turned the corner and headed home.

Tomorrow was Sunday. I spent the remainder of the afternoon prepping for church. Since I had gotten baptized, church attendance was prioritized. I had a small load of clothes to wash, including a dress that I wanted to wear to church, so I got it done.

The sun was still shining brightly, so I hung the clothes on the line outside to dry. I liked the scent of the clothes after they dried in the sun. I also enjoyed folding them as neatly as possible.

Tidiness and neatness were very important to me, and I took pride in doing so. I also looked forward to the compliments that

Daddy gave when he noticed something about me that impressed him.

Oh, how I looked forward to hearing him use words such as "Industrious, studious, well done, and fantastic." 'Till this day, I still cannot articulate why my father's words resonated with me so deeply. Something divine, I suppose.

The clothes dried, and it was time to follow up with ironing. The tan, gray, and white Sunday dress complemented the warm, beautiful Jamaican summer.

The laced trim, coupled with a wide collar, brought back childhood memories of wearing my Sunday's best to special church functions. The silky white pair of leggings was a perfect match for the white pair of low pumps that were given to me as a gift.

The bunned hairstyle was common. It was most convenient when I did not have to wear the long, weighted, below-the-shoulder lengthened hair. The extreme heat did not help.

The little clutch purse proved loyal over the years. It was time to head to the small, holy church that I had gotten baptized in, but not before I grabbed the Bible.

The Bible was my closest asset between God and me, aside from the church. It was life or death, in my view, to not have my Bible with me.

Before I left for church, I said goodbye to Ms. Manning. She was getting ready to attend the Anglican Church where she was an estoute member.

Only the "elites" went to that church, in my opinion, and I was certainly not anywhere close to being one, and I highly doubted that I would have felt comfortable in such a class.

CHAPTER 8: A SUNDAY WALK AND INNER BATTLES

The walk to church was pleasant. The morning sun seemed to grace the community with its gentle rays as if to say, I am only here for a bit.

Creations such as the sun, birds, and flowers, for instance, began to take on a new look since I decided to venture on a Christian journey. There was an unexplained appreciation for things that I normally took for granted.

I grew up in a culture that was filled with the most natural beauties that were created. For instance, located just below the home where I spent most of my childhood was the Rio Minho River.

It was utilized for many purposes by my family. My family utilized it for washing clothes, cooking, bathing, fishing, and feeding the animals. It was also used for picnicking or family gatherings where cooking and music were common, especially during holidays.

Exotic fruit trees such as mangoes, cherries, oranges, and guineps were plentiful for the community. The produce from those trees and numerous more were daily meals for the residents.

Vegetations such as cabbage, potatoes, and callaloo were used to prepare daily meals for families.

The blooming flowers, such as daffodils, Blue Mahoes, and Hibiscus, graced the fields and sidewalks, producing a tranquil atmosphere for passersby.

Natural beauties such as these were overlooked as necessities; instead, they were viewed as common and that they would always be there.

The sun on this Sunday, however, was saying something differently. It was telling me not to take it for granted.

It was speaking to me in a most unusual way that I could not articulate. Maybe it was saying that nothing was forever? That it may rain? Or that it may be covered by clouds?

Whatever it was saying, I could tell that things, as I saw them, were temporary.

The voices in my head seemed to be conflicting with each other as though there was a war or battle going on, and each side wanted to win by any means.

It was as though two worlds had been erected, and I was the only resident of both worlds. Interestingly frightening.

In one world, I was a college grad with great expectations from my father and my culture.

In the other, I was faced with a supernatural world that was challenging everything in the world that I had grown up in.

The land, natural resources, family, friends, and even my father's and my cultural expectations were all of a sudden being challenged.

I did not know how to react to what was going on in my thoughts. I could not walk away from it either, and it was too strange to discuss with anyone.

Since I was separated from my siblings at an early age, I morphed into independence, which isolated me from almost everyone, so I essentially had no one to confide in about what I was experiencing.

There was a dear friend whom I had met in grade 5. We had not kept in touch due to the fluidity of my living arrangements.

Staying connected by wave links such as cell phones or home phones was not an option because they were unavailable in the rural areas of Jamaica at that time.

Writing letters was an option, but the delay in mail delivery was not motivating and proved futile at times.

The only valid options were visitations by public transportation.

Only the well-to-dos had private vehicles, and I did not fall into that category.

I never thought that Daddy would have allowed me to visit my dear friend because he had doubts about my visiting some of my own family members, much less a friend.

I did not bother to ask him.

I looked at the clock. As I got ready to attend church, contrary thoughts rocked my brain.

Shyness was not a part of my personality. Respect was, especially for persons in certain roles.

A pastor, for instance, held the highest respect, at least in my view.

Every other role or governance was due theirs, but not those who proclaim to be Christians.

As the thoughts battled with each other in my mind, I wrestled with whether I should talk with the pastor or one of the church members about what was happening to me.

It was 10:00 AM. Church services commenced at 10:30 AM.

Sunday schools for both the children and the adults were in session in separate areas of the main sanctuary.

Respectfully and quietly, as the customs called for, I joined the group after kneeling down to pray for safe travels.

One must never interrupt the lessons being taught, so no verbal greetings were exchanged, only nods of acknowledgment.

A dear sister in Christ, as those who were baptized were addressed, slid me a note of the scriptures that were being read.

I quickly joined in with the reading, but nothing was resonating.

The battle in my head that I had on the way to church was still going on.

I wanted to interrupt the Sunday school teacher and ask her if she could help, but I was too afraid to do so.

Praying was not a practice of mine.

I did not know how to pray because I did not know if God would hear me.

I had not seen Him.

I did not know if He truly existed.

I was lost in my thoughts.

I got up and went to the restroom that was detached from the main building.

I needed a quiet place to gather myself.

I must have spent about 20 minutes just thinking to myself.

I felt alone.

I remembered saying to myself that if only I could stop that strong desire to understand or know this God, the Creator of all the created things that I had seen since I was a child.

I could not deny that there was something or someone greater than my own father, a man whom I thought the world of.

It was almost as though that person was a threat to daddy's role, and it scared me to give my allegiance to someone other than daddy.

The war in my head was almost unbearable.

I decided to leave the church early.

I needed to get back home to my room and think.

I needed complete quietness.

On the way home, I began reflecting on my life.

"Winsome, you must not have a boyfriend. Boyfriends create babies, and babies need care, "Daddy warned.

"You must get your education first. Business before pleasure," he continued.

I had never seen my dad go to church, but he was so principled; I could not deny him.

I wondered if I had done everything that Daddy wanted me to do.

I wondered if I had honored the scriptures that I had heard in church that state that children should obey their parents so that their lives will be long upon the earth.

I wondered if I was obeying God.

All of a sudden, it became clear to me that the inner struggle was about my allegiance.

An allegiance from my earthly father to the Spiritual Father.

The very thought of switching allegiances was scary and troubling.

I could not explain what was happening to me, and why, but there was a desperate desire to understand.

I got home around noon.

I greeted Ms. Manning, and the housekeeper retired to my room for the early part of the afternoon.

I closed the bedroom door and placed the Bible on the nightstand and my purse on the dresser.

Staring into space, I sat on the edge of the bed.

I began questioning the revelation I had on the way home from church.

The revelation of allegiance.

What did that mean, I asked myself.

Why was the pressure about this so strong? I questioned myself.

Ideally, speaking to the pastor of the church about the battle that I was struggling with would have probably helped, but I had become a member for only a short time.

The community, including the church, was fairly new to me.

Except for a dear cousin whose family had relocated there for only a short time, I knew of no one else.

The thought came to me to disclose to Ms. Manning what was happening to me, but I figured that she would think that I was hallucinating or something.

I did not feel comfortable talking to anyone but Daddy about my dilemma.

CHAPTER 9: TALKING WITH DADDY

The following day was Monday. Mondays were not my usual days to visit Daddy. Wednesdays were.

I woke up at about 8:00 AM, brushed my teeth, showered, and got dressed. It was customary to tidy my room, so I did, including making up the bed. I wasn't starving, so I used the kettle to boil some water, made a cup of mint tea, and ate a few water crackers.

Next, I collected my purse and headed out of the gate. Ms. Manning was still asleep, so I gently closed the gate behind me. I did not feel up to taking the 15-minute walk to daddy's job, so I summoned one of the taxies that normally parked in the subdivision. Within a few minutes, I was in town.

I hurried into the station where Daddy was ending his night shift. He seemed surprised to see me, but accommodated my company nonetheless. He beckoned for me to sit in the designated area until he gathered his belongings. A few minutes later, we were walking out the exit.

"So, Winnie, I am surprised to see you. Are you alright?" he asked.

Before I could respond to daddy's question, I recalled that the name Winnie brought back memories when daddy used it to address me as a gesture of closeness or oneness, I supposed. Winnie is short for Winsome, which is the name that daddy named me, which is symbolic of his middle name, Winston.

"I think so, Daddy," I responded. "There is something that I am struggling with that I would like to talk with you about," I continued.

Across from the station was a public park that Dad and I frequented when we wanted to hang out and eat a beef patty or drink a Ting.

"Alright, let's go to the park and talk," said Daddy.

We found a park bench in close proximity to the park's stand-alone clock tower. We decided to use that one. Daddy and I sat about two feet apart on the bench. He postured towards my direction at a 180-degree angle. His facial expression was solemn and questionable.

Daddy rarely, if ever, showed any emotions, so I could not detect what his feelings were as he waited to hear what I had to say.

"Daddy, do you remember when I told you that I was going to join the church that is in the community and that I was planning to be baptized?" I asked.

"Yes, I do," he replied.

"Well, I did. I knew that you had little interest in the church practices, so I did not bother to elaborate about my experiences, and I kept them to myself," I continued.

"On my way to church yesterday, I had an encounter or a situation that won't allow me to focus or be restless," I said.

"Tell me about it," Daddy replied.

"I will try to, daddy, but I do not know if I will confuse you," I replied.

"It is very confusing to me," I continued.

"Alright, let's talk about it," said Daddy.

Daddy's legs were now crossed at his ankles, and his hands clasped and placed slightly above his knees. I had seen that posture many times during important discussions or conversations, such as when he was introducing me to my new landlords at the boarding houses. He was poised to hear what I had to say.

For the next 20-25 minutes, I vented to my father. I told him that I was afraid. That I must have made a mistake in joining the church. I told him that I felt like I was losing my allegiance to him and that I did not know how he would feel about it.

I also told him that I wanted to ask him about the trip to America, but I did not want to thwart his future plans for me. Also, I revealed to him that I wanted to date because I was 19 years old and had graduated from school, just as he had wanted me to.

Crying was not a common practice for me, but I broke. I cried in the presence of my father, whom I had never seen crying, nor have I cried in front of him. Then he replied.

Over the next hour or so, Daddy revealed his most intimate experiences and thoughts to me. Things that I needed to hear so that I could become whole.

He told me that he grew up as a church boy and that he was a Sunday school teacher. His mother had passed away when he was quite young, so he was raised by his aunt, his mother's sister.

His aunt was a loyal church attendee who served in the ministry, and so he, Daddy, was expected to follow suit. He met my mother when he was a young adult. They got married and had children. He and my mother were both involved in the church and took part in Sunday school functions and activities.

After he joined the police academy, he was sent for training, and he stopped attending church due to his duty schedules. Daddy also revealed to me that although he liked serving his community as a police officer, he carried a sense of guilt or regret that he had turned away from the church in such a fashion.

He also said that the decision I made to be baptized was profound and that he thought that I had begun a new journey.

"I don't understand what you mean by a new journey, daddy," I said. "What do you mean?" I asked.

"I was on that journey after I was baptized when I was a young boy. By journey, I mean that you will be transformed in Christ's image according to the scriptures so that you can live a life that is pleasing to Jesus. That transformation happens by the Holy Spirit revealing Himself to you through the written word of God. That is why you are experiencing what you are, and it feels strange," said Daddy.

"Winnie, I have taken you as far as I can. You must pave your own path now. This is why I am sending you to America. I pray that God will guide and protect you always," said Daddy.

"Do not be afraid of losing your allegiance to me. I will always be here when you need me. I am sending you to my dear friend, who will do what I have asked him to. May God be with you," said Daddy.

The conversation had ended between Daddy and me. He patted my shoulder as a gesture of reassurance. Hugging was not customary in Jamaican culture, but any form of gentle, comforting touch from a parent was assumed as a good sign. Our meeting had ended.

The mid-morning was exceptionally pleasant. I watched my dad walk to his motorcycle and cranked it. He drove away at a slower pace than normal. A pace that resonated captured thoughts.

Daddy was not known to be repetitive. I knew that the conversation that we just had was "written in stone." He meant what he said.

My body and soul suddenly felt free and lighter. I felt like I could jump up and down because of the relief that daddy granted me. I was not crazy. I was not weird. Daddy had experienced the same sort of transformation and it was okay.

With elation, I walked across the street from the park to grab a bite. I had a taste for jerked pork and ginger beer. The taste of ginger beer-carbonated water would suffice the sudden thirst and tightened stomach that I had earlier that morning.

As I sat in the restaurant, I began reflecting on the memories that I had in the town of Chapelton. I spent most of my school days in that city either shopping at the market, going to school, visiting my father who worked at the only police station in that town, waiting for public transportations to transport me to various locations from that hub, or even visiting the local hospital in that town.

The jerk pork, red beans/rice and raw veggies gave me a boost of energy, so I decided to do some exploration of the town while summer gave me the opportunity. In retrospect, I must've had some sort of intuition because I did not know that it would have taken over a decade to return to that town after I had gone to America.

CHAPTER 10: A WALK AROUND TOWN

I exited the restaurant and headed south on foot towards the hospital. When I was a young girl, I dreamt of becoming a nurse. The desire came from the hope of helping the wounded.

I recalled standing at the public transportation main loading area in the town. It was within walking distance of the hospital. I remembered seeing many patients wearing bandages on their arms or legs, and I felt sorry for them. I wanted to help them. I would fantasize about cleaning their wounds, applying first aid, and then bandaging the wounded areas, and they would be okay.

I took the first right turn from the main road that led to the hospital. As I passed the hardware store on the left, I made eye contact with one of my schoolmates. She was with her mother. We waved at each other and went our separate ways.

The quarter-mile walk from the main road to the hospital was pleasant. I passed by a private home, situated on the left, that I was always curious about. It nestled behind the most luscious trees and was gated all around. I wondered who resided there each time I passed by throughout the years. I never found out.

I was on the hospital grounds. I took the liberty of going up the steps and around the back of the main building. I wanted to be up close and personal, almost embodying what the hospital represented, which was making patients well again.

For privacy reasons, I could not visit the patients without being a family member and being granted permission, so I simply walked along the premises and took in as much as I could.

The exterior of the building was neatly maintained. The nurses hustled along in their all-white attire as though they were on a mission. There was no time for casual conversations, I discerned, so I did not bother to interrupt them.

As I exited the grounds of the hospital, I glanced upstairs to see if I could spot the faithful doctor, Dr. Lindo. He was known to almost every local, and his good reputation went a long way throughout the many years that he served the community. He reminded me a bit of my father due to their very mild demeanors. I did not see him, so I continued down the path to the local library.

The library was located within a 12-minute walk from the hospital. I frequented it numerous times to do research or just to hang out while I was attending Clarendon College (CC), since CC was within a 20-25-minute walk from the library.

Though I was not allowed to have a boyfriend, and I had gotten baptized, I could not help wondering what it must've been like hanging out with a boy like the other girls that I would see doing at the library. I never found out.

I recalled a decent, handsome Christian young man who lived southeast of Chapelton, about 7 miles from the town where I resided for about 4 years. We casually met each other in passing. He and his friend would often visit the town where my sister and I resided.

There was a soccer (Jamaican football) field close by, and Sunday evenings drew large crowds to watch the locals play. That young man, his friend, and my sister would chat until late in the afternoons. Oh, how I enjoyed those conversations! He eventually joined the army, and we lost touch with each other. He was dearly missed.

As I looked at those girls and boys hanging out with each other at the library, I felt a bit jealous, but happy simultaneously, because it seemed that they were enjoying each other's company while I could only dream.

The library was filled with informational materials. Donations were often made from the well-to-dos, so the learning materials remained relevant.

There was one area that I found relaxing, and it was in the corner to the right of the main study lounge. It had enough space for one, and I had grown accustomed to enjoying my own company due to numerous relocations with boarding where I was the only teenager in those homes.

I settled in that 5X8 space and read or wrote until I had had enough. The librarian was very accommodating, and she ensured that the visitors could spend their time in peace. That was a plus.

Before I left the compound, I walked outside on the manicured lawn and sat under the shade of the cedar tree. The surroundings exuded a sense of tranquility that was captivating. I did not want to leave. It was close to 11:00 AM, and I had a few more stops to make before I headed home.

The sun was shining in all its glory as I exited the library's grounds. I did not mind the intense summer heat because I had something to be thankful for, and it was seeing the world through a new lens, thanks to my father. I had decided to seize each moment by paving my own path, according to my daddy's advice.

It was almost lunch time, and the smell of curry sauce and grilling smoke was in the air. I was not starving, but I could eat something light. Maybe a beef patty.

Ms. Linda's home was not too far away from where I was. I decided to knock on the gate to see if anyone was home. Ms. Linda was a most charming woman whom Daddy met through his affiliation with the judicial system.

Ms. Linda entertained the officiating judge who presided over the courthouse where Daddy was a security guard on Wednesdays during trials. I boarded with her for a short time. She was very kind to me. Her beautiful 2,200 square feet home nestled on a light slope off the main highway that ran through Chapelton town. My room was located on the left side of the home with an adjoining full bath. The comfort of the home signified the beautiful spirit that Ms. Linda possessed.

I knocked on the gate three times, but no one answered. Then someone opened the door of the residence. He immediately recognized who I was and asked me if I was there to visit Ms. Linda. I told him yes.

He told me that she had gone to America to visit with her son and would be returning at the end of July. It was mid-June. The young man was overseeing the property while Ms. Linda was abroad, a common practice among Jamaican homeowners. I recalled Daddy being left to oversee a number of homes while the owners travelled. Trust was a requirement, and Daddy seemed to be trusted.

I thanked the young man and asked him to tell Ms. Linda that I had stopped by. I continued walking.

As I passed by Mr. Lee's grocery store, I stopped in to say hello to my morning buddy, B. B. His parents owned the grocery store, and he ran its operations. While I was boarding with Ms. Linda, I attended Beulah All Age School. The school was about 5 miles from Chapelton, so I relied on the public transportation to transport me to school.

B would stand at the front of the shop, and we would chit-chat until transportation arrived. He was pleasant to converse with.

"Winsome. How are you?" asked B.

"I am alright. I wanted to say hello to you before I go home."

"Oh, alright. What will you be doing for the summer?" he asked.

"Oh, daddy is sending me away to America,' I replied.

"Really?"

"I have some relatives there. They like it over there. When are you leaving?" he continued.

"Next month," I replied.

"Have a good time," he responded.

"Thank you," I replied.

CHAPTER 11: VISITING CC AND HEADING TO THE FARM

The walk to CC from Mr. Lee's shop was about 12 minutes. I wanted to drop by and look at the campus one last time while on summer break, and to say hello to my cousins, the Myers, who worked in administration.

The afternoon weather was steamy, but tolerable. It had rained the night before, so the climate was a bit humid. Hurricane season was upon us, so toting an umbrella was not a bad idea in case it rained unexpectedly.

The entrance gate to Clarendon College was closed. A security guard stood up and greeted me. He asked for a few credentials, then allowed me to enter. The walk from the gate to the buildings took another 3 or so minutes. The theme colors of pale yellow and blue graced the buildings in an artistic presentation.

I walked toward the back of the campus on the left, towards the administrative offices. The campus had an eerie feeling of emptiness that felt uneasy. No more hustling and bustling of students going about their business. Rightly so. They had worked diligently for 10 months, and it was time for a break.

In the distance, I saw a petite, framed woman who looked like my cousin. As I got closer, I realized that it was her. Her smile could brighten anyone's day. We greeted each other with the warmest smiles, chatted for a bit, and said our goodbyes.

I continued to the classrooms where I had spent so many months learning new things. I could not enter due to summer cleaning. As I stood on the concrete platform, I began reminiscing.

Mathematics and I did not get along when I was attending

Beulah All Age and May Pen Secondary. As a matter of fact, I recalled my math teacher, Mr. M, calling me up to the blackboard to work out a problem, and I froze. The strangest thing was, when I was seated, I got the hang of the examples that Mr. He worked on the board, but when I stood in front of the class to demonstrate what I knew, I could not.

I concluded that I was scared of both math and dozens of eyes looking at me at the same time. At CC, something clicked. Maybe it was the teacher, the environment of just maturity, but mathematics became my favorite subject. I could do Algebraic expressions in my sleep. I am joking.

Clarendon College was not just a place of academic excellence; it prepared me for the real world. The sports organization was a huge part of CC's culture. Football was the most popular. Many games were held on the campus's field, located just below the hill.

The staff and students looked forward to fun times on Friday evenings on the field. The array of blue, yellow, and white of the uniforms signified unity and strength because we were victorious in most of our championship games. We earned bragging rights, for sure!

As I left the campus toward home, I got tickled thinking of a couple of prefect boys who had a crush on me. Cute. I admired their intelligence, and that was where it stopped. One was brave enough to ask my father if I could be his girlfriend. I knew the response to that, so I did not get my hopes up. As a matter of fact, I didn't think that we would have lasted in a relationship because he was too stiff and I was a happy-go-lucky kind of gal.

It was 1:00 pm. I had had a very productive half a day and was on my way back home. I was a bit tired from walking the 25-minute walk down the hill to my house, so I called for a taxi.

I greeted Ms. Manning as she sat on the veranda and then headed to my room. I jumped in the shower and then went to sleep. I was tired. I woke up around 5:00 pm and ate supper. I chatted with Ms. Manning until around 8:00 pm. Afterwards, I brushed my teeth and then read a couple of Bible scriptures.

Yesterday was a great day. Got a lot accomplished that I wanted to before the trip. It was the middle of June. The trip to America was scheduled for July 9, which was about 3 weeks away.

Mother lived about 40 minutes away, and I wanted to visit with her before I left the island. It was the beginning of the week, and I wanted to visit her on the weekend. Now that I was older, I wanted to have a heart-to-heart conversation with her.

My memories of her prior to her leaving the island for about ten years were surprisingly intact. I must've been between the ages of 8 and 10-years-old.

Mother was a warrior, at least from my perspective. She was a stay-at-home mother, but stay-at-home took on a different meaning when it came to her. When she met my father, she had told me during one of our rare, but significant talks, that she inherited the farm as well, which my father inherited from his grandfather. The farm became a source of household necessities. She spent a great deal of time in the coffee walk reaping coffee to sell at the local market. I recalled my older brother and I going to the farm with her on one of her many trips. I must have been about 7 years old.

Trips to the farm must take place during the peak of dawn because of the distance, and one needs to avoid the scorching sun, which peaks around 1:00 pm. Mother woke us up around 5 or 6:00 am. She had prepared a cup of mint tea and egg sandwiches for breakfast.

Our home was not equipped with a modern-day kitchen and stove. The kitchen was detached from the main residence and was not equipped with electricity. It was made of cedar wood, zinc, and bamboo. An elevated grill made of concrete and steel was where all meals were prepared, except for occasional stovepot camping style.

The kettle that was used to boil water was worn out, but useful nonetheless. The mint tea and egg sandwich were delicious. Mother could use anything to make a meal, and it was a 5-star rating for sure.

It was time for us to head to the farm. Mother told us to put on our farm clothing for a reason. The farm was located across the river and up the steep slope. Mosquitos were terrible, and we risked getting several bites before returning home.

In those days, children had only three distinct categories of clothing: church, school, and judging or around-the-house types of attire. We all geared up in clothing for combating all of the natural elements that we were about to experience.

It was time to head out. My brother was a year older. The responsibility of climbing trees for fruits and digging yams or potatoes, for example, rested on him. He took a machete with him and a crocus bag. A machete was a vital tool for farming because it served numerous purposes.

My brother needed it to clear the bushy parts so that we could walk without much obstruction. He also needed it to cut banana stalks to access bananas that were used for preparing meals, and chipping coconuts. A coconut served multiple purposes, such as providing nutrient-packed water. It also produced a jelly or solid substance for quick meals, and the dry carcass was used as a burning substance for camp-style cooking.

On our journey, we passed by a mango tree. There were mangoes on the ground from an overload of the limbs, so my brother picked up the only one that did not seem to have worms. As he sliced it open with the machete, it fell out of his hands.

The most interesting thought immediately ran through my mind. "Why did God cause the mango to drop from my brother's hand?" I questioned myself. I still do not know why I had that question. Was it because, in some way, I knew that He could have prevented the mango from falling? Or was it because we really wanted to taste such a pretty mango?

The journey from home to the farm was a 20-30 minute walk to the top of the hill. Mother directed from the back as she instructed my brother on what to do. As the oldest son, he was being prepared to take over the family farm as the culture allowed, so mother was preparing him.

Mother had a toughness about her that seemed to be fearless. She was known as the woman who caught fish with her mouth in one of the deepest parts of the Rio Minho River. Her determination to feed her children put her in some of the most challenging places: it was incredible.

As we journeyed down the steep, bushy hill towards the river, she advised my brother and me to hold on to the bushes and to look carefully as we walked. If we had made any huge mistakes, there was a possibility of us falling into the river at the foot of the hill.

We finally got to the foot of the hill, and it was time to cross the river or climb a rock to get to the family farm. Mother chose to cross the river, so she led by placing one foot forward to determine which area was deep or shallow.

CHAPTER 12: COFFEE BEANS, CLOSE CALLS, AND MOTHER'S STRENGTH

We came to the bottom of the hill that led to the family farm. The coffee trees were about fifty feet up and over on the right of the farm. Mother and I went to pick the ripened coffee beans while my brother went to dig the yams and collected other foods to prepare dinner once we got back home.

Mother had brought a large bin for the coffee beans to be placed in. As she and I began picking the beans, the mosquitoes swarmed us. Mosquitoes love moist, warm, watery areas, and such were the conditions in that area. We had no choice but to fight back, so we began hitting them with our clothing, leaves, or whatever else was there. They were persistent, but we managed to pick half a bin in a short time, which was awesome!

It was almost midday, and we began preparing to take the long, treacherous journey back home. My brother was on top of the hill on the other side of the farm. Mother sent me to let him know that it was time to prepare for home.

As I got close to my brother, my foot slipped, and I began falling. Out of nowhere, my brother grabbed my hand and held it as I swung in the open air. Mother heard us crying out for help. I could hear her running up the hill towards us as the dry leaves from the trees smashed beneath her feet.

She managed to snatch me from my brother's hand and placed me next to her. I do not know what a near-death experience is, but I must've come close to it twice, and that moment was one of them. The other time was while I was living with my cousin in Chapelton Four Paths, which is a community located about 40 minutes from Kraal. I was riding in a car on my way home from school. As the driver entered the top of the main road that led to my cousin's house, the car became airborne from the rainy road and rested on a slope. If the car had fallen off, no one would have survived.

Those two close calls not only caused great fear, but they also caused me to wonder how such close moments did not turn out differently. I wondered if it was God who spared my life. I knew nothing about God for myself, so I could not come to a finality about the situations.

Mother's eyes sparkled with weariness and gratitude, it appeared. She cautiously escorted my brother and me to the lower part of the hill. We gathered the day's harvest and headed towards the river and up the hill to the main road that led home.

Mother's toughness and bravery reminded me of the Arawak Indians of Jamaica, her ancestors. She protected me from being raped, I recalled. I was on my way home from school. The walk home was on the main road, not too far from Mango Walk.

As I went around the bend, I heard noises coming from a large grassy plant on the side of the road behind me. I turned around to see what caused the sound—a man dashed out of the grass and tried to grab me. I ran all the way home and told my mother what had happened.

I recalled her taking her long, Indian hair and rolling it on top of her head as she headed in the same direction I had just come from. She walked all the way to the place where I had the encounter. She looked around with a machete in her hand as she lamented for whoever it was to come forth.

From the look in her eyes and the sound of her voice, there was no telling what she would have done with the machete had she seen the person. She reported the incident to the local police, who found the man and arrested him on attempted rape charges.

As I reflected on that close moment, I wondered how I was able to run that fast and long away from someone who was probably three times my height and age. I wondered about God.

Mother was a very kind person. Our family consisted of eight. Preparing meals was not an easy task due to the amount of labor to get to the farm and the lack of amenities to cook the meals. Sometimes there was barely enough food for the family, much less to share. Yet, mother was able to share with anyone who strayed onto the property. It was incredible.

She always had something to offer anyone who may be tired on the way home from farming, or for anyone who needed to rest from a long day's journey on foot. In those days, mail delivery was by foot. There was a man who literally delivered mail to residences. Mother would always have some water or food for him as he made his routes.

The weekend had arrived, and I was off to visit mother. As I walked past the only church in the community, memories from childhood rushed through my thoughts. I wondered if Pastor Dilan was still pastoring, I thought. I wondered if Sunday school for the children was still being held.

I enjoyed Sunday school because it was fun to be with the other children. Reciting scriptures and sitting obediently during the sermon were two things that I enjoyed, strangely.

I glanced just below the church onto the other side of the road. The mango tree where my brother dropped his mango was still there.

As I walked towards my mother's residence, I said hello to the neighbors. They all seemed to have a bright smile. I was finally at the gate and on my way up the house, which was nestled on a little hill.

"Winsome, a you dat?" asked mother in her Jamaican dialect.

"Yes, mommy, it's me," I replied. We welcomed each other with a warm embrace.

Mother was washing clothes and hanging them on the clothesline outside. A pot of beef soup was boiling on the stove. The spicy-scented aroma filled the atmosphere with an inviting presence that attracted even the passersby.

Saturdays were typically vibrant in the small district. Music could be heard playing at the residential houses. Long-time traditions. The district was lively and vibrant, and the residents would have settled for nothing less.

"Are you hungry, Winsome?" my mother asked.

"Yes, mommy, I am," I responded.

"I will prepare some soup for us. We will sit on the bamboo bench in the front of the yard," she said.

"Yes, Mommy," I said. The domesticated cats and dogs were waiting patiently for any food that was given to them. The background music was relaxing.

I placed my overnight bag on the veranda, then I went to help my mother prepare the soup. We were now seated and getting ready to enjoy the delicious meal.

"How have you been, Winsome?" asked my mother. "We have not seen each other since the baptism," she continued. "How are things going with that?" she asked.

"Yes, mommy. We have not. Things are different, very different since the baptism," I replied.

"Well, how so?" she asked. Before I could elaborate, mother interrupted with a chuckle. That chuckle was synonymous with her personality.

You see, mother had a unique, sarcastic humor about her that resonated through her eyes. It was as though she could tell what I was thinking before I spoke. Intuition or experience, I guessed. Whatever it was, it must've been likened to a divine gift.

She had 10 children, and she knew each of our personalities, and she was spot on. When she was approached by any of us, we automatically knew that mother expected nothing but respect, no matter the age.

The very look in her eyes warned us to be as real and authentic as possible because she could discern a lie from the truth, or pretence from authenticity. For the next hour or so, mother bellowed out her thoughts in an uncut, genuine fashion.

CHAPTER 13: MOTHER'S LESSONS AND SUNDAY STROLLS

Mother began the conversation by talking about her experience as a Sunday school teacher. She and my father met and were married sometime after. During the courting period, they both became members of a church where they took part as Sunday school teachers. Shortly after, my mother conceived, but she and my father were unwed at the time. Due to the customs of the church organization, they could not continue their roles in the church, so they stepped down. They eventually left the organization and the practices. "If I knew that life would be this difficult, I would have stayed in the church," she reflected. Mother admonished me to continue on the path of the Christian faith. "Read the Bible and continue attending church," she continued.

I did not feel a need to interrupt; I just wanted to listen to wise counsel, at least that's what I called mother's admonition. She advised me to pray when I got discouraged and to seek help when I needed it. She encouraged me to continue obeying my father because he had good intentions.

"Has he told you about the trip?" I asked.

"Yes, he did," she responded. "Your father and I may not be together, but I know that he cares for you," she said.

After a lengthy and informative conversation, we decided to take a walk to the junction. The junction was situated in the middle of the town square. It was a social gathering place for the residents. There, the neighbors got a chance to mingle with each other while enjoying lovely snacks from the local shops, along with listening to music playing in the background.

The 5-minute stride was pleasant. Mother and I casually chatted as we walked. The fruit trees were laden with fruit and the birds, goats, and humans did not waste any time devouring the ripened ones. Social gatherings were the highlights of the community because everyone seemed to forget their problems, if it were even for the evening.

Two hours of social gathering and fun had passed. Mother and I headed back home. I showered and headed to bed.

The next day was Sunday. I brought a Sunday dress for church. I wanted to rest well, so I recited the Our Father prayer and got into bed. There were no alarms, so I relied on the roosters to wake me up so that I would not miss Sunday school.

As a child, reciting the studied Bible scriptures was the highlight of the day. At the end of each Sunday, each Sunday school participant was given up to three Bible verses to study for the following Sunday. The teacher called on each child to recite his or her assigned scriptures without any errors. If we made any mistakes during the recital, we were given the same scriptures to restudy until we got them correct.

In retrospect, the practice seemed harsh, but as a teenager, I could appreciate the practice as it related to real-life application.

It was 9:00 am. Sunday services began at 10:00 am. The distance between home and church was less than a 5-minute walk. Mother hustled up and prepared fitters, ackee & salted, and coco tea for breakfast. One of my favourites.

During breakfast, I asked her if she was going to church as well. I kinda suspected her response would be a no. After breakfast, I brushed my teeth, showered, and got dressed.

It would not have mattered how many times I showered; the

intense sun rays caused the dress to cling to my slightly damp body as I made my way down the slope from the yard to the church. Thank goodness that the colors of the dress were earth-toned, so I did not have to worry about the light perspiration being obvious.

Customarily, church attire must represent cleanliness and wholesomeness, and I did not want the mothers of the church to reprimand me.

Upon entering the sanctuary, I noticed that prayer was in session. Respectfully, according to the customs, I instantly knelt and joined in the prayer. Five minutes passed, and Sunday school had begun.

As expected, the children gathered in the same place where I did as a child. The same practices were practiced, and the same pastor acknowledged the procedure. Seeing that, I was emotionally charged.

The memories came rushing back. Memories such as the satisfaction I got when I saw the Sunday school teacher or the pastor nod in acknowledgement to a job well done. Or, the relief we felt when each child recited his scriptures accurately.

It was as though we were aiming for a prize that was impossible to attain; yet, hope remained relevant.

I joined the adults' Sunday school program, where I was instantly assigned a role: the scripture reading. Once I read the scriptures, elaboration was expected. Each person took turns and gave his opinion until the end of the program.

We closed the session with a prayer, then joined the congregation for the sermon.

"Do not do anything that will send you to hell," I recalled the sermon being about. The word hell became a frightening word in my thoughts.

Throughout most of my childhood years, that topic was preached on more than anything else that I could remember. It caused tremendous fear in me, so much so that I did everything to not go to that dreadful place.

Four things I had to remember not to do to avoid going to hell were no drinking alcohol, no premarital sex, no smoking, and no lying. If I could just somehow avoid these four categories, I would be okay, were my thoughts.

I set out to do those things with all my might. The pastor's facial expression while preaching on the topic of hell was most convincing. He was a man who had been in the pulpit for a number of years. His reputation was flawless in the community, and his humility was incredible.

There was no reason to doubt such a messenger of God, according to the expectations and traditions of religious practices, from what I had observed. A preacher, you see, was the closest messenger to God.

When he spoke, people listened. If people did the opposite of what the preacher said, they were doomed to hell. That was the stance that many people took and lived by accordingly.

I adopted that point of view as a child. As a 19-year-old, I still believed it. I had not read the Bible enough for myself, nor did I even know that I had permission to. It was almost understood that only the pastor heard from God. No one else did.

Throughout the sermon, I observed others, especially the more seasoned or mature members, cheering on the pastor as a sign of acknowledgement and agreement to everything that he preached.

It was most fascinating to witness the unity amongst everyone.

Meanwhile, I struggled to wrap my mind around those four sinful acts. From a teenager's point of view, condemnation was a constant in my life. The very thought of lying scared me, so I willfully avoided situations where I would be forced to tell a lie.

I was having a difficult time trying to live up to those rules. As a child, I recalled my mother smoking while she stood inside the outdoor kitchen. She was standing behind the kitchen door.

Customarily, children were almost forbidden to question their parents about any decisions that they made, but somehow, I managed to ask my mother why she was standing behind the kitchen door.

Her response was, "I am hiding from God because I don't want him to see me smoking."

That response has stuck in my memory since I was 5-years-old.

In retrospect, my mother also believed that smoking would lead her to hell. At that time, she was not a church attendee, but it was quite obvious that she was convinced of its practices.

CHAPTER 14: SUNDAY REFLECTIONS AND COMMUNITY LIFE

Church services ended, and it was time to go home. The 5-minute walk home seemed like 50-minutes. There were so many questions on my mind about salvation, faith, religion, or whatever term was placed on living right to avoid hell. There was no one to talk to about such a topic because everyone's view was the same. After all, they were doing their best to walk the straight and narrow and would probably not have wanted to be burdened with a barrage of questions from a teenager.

Daddy had already given me his viewpoint about my newly found path. I felt tremendous guilt and condemnation before God because, for some odd reason, I believed my father's viewpoint over the pastor's. I wanted to keep it a secret because I was afraid, like my mother, that God would be angry with me.

Mother was home preparing dinner. I knew not to delve into the questions that I had with her because she had already given me her views. The only person left to ask these questions was me. God would have been ideal to answer them, but from what was preached, he was somewhere in heaven, and heaven to me was somewhere in the sky, and there was no way I could get there to sit down and have a conversation with him.

By the time I turned 19-years of age, I had visited more than four churches. In each recalled sermon, God was presented as being very far away. He was unreachable not to only me, but to the preachers and fellow believers.

I was now facing one thought process that I did not want to face, and that thought process was getting away from everything that I learned about God. It was the most troubling, thought-provoking thought that I had, but it was as though that was my only option.

I was a 19-year-old who was getting ready to go on adventure hundreds of miles away to a place where I had never been, and to someone whom I had only met in passing. Away from everything that formed me, especially my father. It was now time to "grow up" and growing up would take on a new challenge. A challenge that included finding out about God in a way that made sense to me. Those were my thoughts, at least.

I made it to my mother's house. She had prepared her famous curried chicken, beans with rice, blended carrots with cabbage, and soursop juice for dinner.

We reclined on the bamboo bench under the mango tree in the front yard. The bamboo bench heard lots of stories as passersby, and the residents sat on that bench more than any other seats that were available.

The location provided a 180-degree view of the structures, domesticated animals, occupants, and fruits/vegetations that were on the property. It also captured the soft, gentle breeze during those cooler months, which was quite welcoming.

Mother and I chatted casually, rarely discussing the day's church service. It was expected. She did ask, however, about a pastor that she had known who resided not too far away from Kraal, who had been at church.

I told her no. She told me that he was a good preacher and that she had not seen him in a while, and wanted to know if he and his lovely wife had visited.

I suppose that the pastor may have sparked some sort of interest in her faith, and she had hoped to hear him preach again. I glanced at my mother as she seemed to drift off into her own thoughts.

I wanted to ask her what she was thinking about, but respect and boundaries did not allow me to. I suspected that she had regrets. Regrets about her own spiritual journey.

When we were children, my siblings and I would gather at the small dining room table on Sunday evenings. There, mother allowed us to sing gospel songs while my brothers exercised their musical abilities by drumming the table with bare fingers.

We spent hours worshipping the Lord with all our might, singing and drumming until we got tired. Mother enjoyed the moments more than we children. It was as though she was inadvertently living her "missed worship" opportunities through us. That was what I concluded, at least.

As we sat on the bamboo bench, a feeling of deep sadness overcame me. I felt sorrow for my mother because she had convinced herself, it seemed, that her life was in the condition that it was because she had committed at least one of the four major sins.

Dinner ended, and it was time to socialize. Sunday evenings were a time to entertain passersby and socialize. The community contained no more than 1000 residents, and everyone knew each other.

Domino games were an excellent social event for men of the community. Often, the women and children prepared light snacks and drinks for the participants as a crowd gathered to watch. The game began while music played in the background.

As far back as I could remember, one thing that made me happy was seeing others having fun or laughing. It did something to me.

Music and food seemed to bring out the best in people, so when I heard of some kind of entertainment that included both, I imagined people having a good time.

A time when they forgot about life's challenges and lived in the moment. Dancing is a great pastime for some of our guests. My sister and I would sit back and watch others dance in a most dramatic way, and we could not help but enjoy the moments with much laughter.

Dancing was and still is a passion of mine. It causes me to imagine a life filled with no worries as I allow my mind to capture the moment. Thank God for a good imagination (laughter).

The four men at the table seemed to be in deep thought as they slammed the domino pieces as though they were making their mark. The opposing team struck back as the standoff to produce the winning team proceeded.

There were no small talks amongst the players as they challenged each other with playing words that could either be taken as an offense or a challenge. Time would tell.

Twenty minutes or so into the game, a team emerged as the winners. The winners played against another team, and the domino effect continued. Those were good times filled with laughter and memories.

It was almost 5:00 pm and the time had arrived for me to return to Sangster's Heights, the boarding home. I could imagine Ms. Manning sitting on the veranda behind the burglar-barred doors, waiting for my return, as she often did when I visited my mother.

Before I bade mother farewell, she packed a fruit and veggies goody bag for me that she gathered from the property. Mother had inherited the property from her parents.

Before they passed away, they managed to plant the most exotic and plentiful fruit and vegetable plants of all the properties in that community.

From the entrance to the left were gungu, bananas, breadfruits, sugar cane, mango trees, and yams, just to name a few things.

To the right were apples, avocado (pear), oranges, dasheens, and even exotic flowers.

In the back of the property and towards the gully or stream were coffee trees, chocolate or cocoa trees, ackee, plantains, coco, coconut trees, and so much more.

Mother found pleasure in sharing the produce with the community, it seemed.

I was packed, and off I went. I took a taxi all the way to my home, which was about a 30-minute drive.

I was home, and just as I thought, Ms. Manning was sitting on the veranda watching the Sunday evening passersby.

CHAPTER 15: JOURNALS, MEMORIES, AND FAREWELLS

"Good evening, Ms. Manning," I greeted. "Oh, good evening, Winsome," she replied. "How was the weekend with your mum?" she asked. Mum was a term that the British used to address mothers. I was quite familiar with switching between British and Jamaican dialect when I conversed with Ms. Manning since her adult life was spent half and half between Great Britain and Jamaica.

"It went well. I had a really good time, thank you," I responded. "How was church today?" I continued.

"Oh, church service was lovely. We had a few visitors from a branch of our organization. It was quite a delight to have them with us today," replied Ms. Manning.

After chit-chatting with Ms. Manning for a bit, I ate dinner, showered, and retired for the night. Tomorrow, Monday was a new day. I had planned to make the most of the remaining few weeks before I left the island.

I had nothing in particular planned out except preparation for the trip. My lifestyle was fairly simple. I owned fewer than five pairs of shoes, and my school uniforms were not relevant to me anymore. I had about six sets of church attire and a few yard or judging outfits. Packing for America was going to be a breeze.

I decided to use the remainder of the time to journal my thoughts. I must have written over five hundred pages in less than two weeks. The good times and not so good times came flooding back to me. I wrote for days with one pen after another as they ran out of ink.

I recalled writing about being separated from my siblings after our mother left for Canada. We had a very close relationship, and it pained me to be separated from them. Crying was uncommon in our household, so it was not an option.

When mommy and daddy met, mother had three children. They had gone to live with their father after mother and daddy got married. I did not get a chance to mingle with them much since I was much younger than they were.

Mother and Daddy had five children together, and we all lived in the same house until Mother left for Canada. I recalled the pain that I endured after being separated from my three brothers.

My sister and I lived together for a short time, then she and I became separated as well. During those times of separation, I became very sad and lonely.

There were a great deal of provisions at the boarding houses, but not being with my siblings was unbearable. Their lives were pretty tough, and I felt sorrow for them more than for myself.

After my mother migrated to Canada, they were sent to live with other relatives and friends of my parents because daddy's house was still under construction. I often wondered how they were fairing but there was no way of contacting them because they would be relocated depending on the condition that they were in.

The circumstances that befell my sister caused us to be apart from each other, and I did not see her again until after a few years. Loneliness was an unwelcoming reality for me.

Making friends was not a guarantee because I was not settled long enough in any one place to truly establish friendships. I questioned myself on many occasions why I was in such a predicament.

I took comfort in reading the Bible, especially when I was experiencing tough times. When I lived in Chapelton Four Paths with my cousin, I attended the church that was located in the square of the community. It was a beautiful church.

I recalled the scripture: John 3:16. And it read, For God so loved the world that He gave His only begotten Son that whosoever believeth in Him should not perish but have everlasting life (KJV).

This scripture resonated with me for a long time. One day, I decided to reread it in a quiet place.

Throughout the church services that I had gone to, I rarely heard of Jesus being emphasized; it was mainly God that was emphasized. After rereading John 3:16, I took notice of the Son of God. I did not know why I was drawn to His deity, but I was fascinated by knowing why.

As I read the scripture, John 3:16, I wanted to understand why God sent His only Son to die for the world. At that time, I could only relate the love of a son with my mother to my oldest brother, Ucel, mother's first son.

My mother had four girls before she had her first son. He was so loved by her that she addressed him as her "right hand."

In those days, farming was a necessity. From its produce, daily meals were provided, animals were fed, and produce was sold to aid with the daily cost of living, just to name a few things.

It would have been ideal to have heavy machinery to help till the ground and reap the produce, but they were either non-existent or too costly. The only other option was manual labor.

A son was most needed to carry out the labor on the farm. As a matter of fact, many sons did not finish school because they were needed to work on the farm. My brother was one of them.

As I reflected on God's son and His death for the world, it seemed like a fairy tale. It did not seem real. Jesus was not only a son, but He was also God's only son.

Why God would send His only Son to die, I wondered. I wondered what kind of love that was…the kind that would sacrifice a son?

From then, a passion developed in me to seek more, find out more…more about Jesus, God, and whatever else the Christian journey entailed.

The journal or a spiral notebook was filled with words, phrases, and questions that I had to have answered, and I set out to find the answers.

I closed the journal and placed it on the bedhead.

It was a Sunday, a little over a week away from leaving Jamaica. Daddy was coming for dinner on Wednesday, and Mother was going to meet Daddy and me in Chapelton on Friday to see me off.

I was scheduled to leave the following Tuesday, July 9.

I had gone to church and told the members about my departure. At the end of the sermon, I was prayed over with all good wishes. I was going to miss everyone and promised to keep in touch.

After church services, I stopped by my cousin's house, the one with the physical impediment. I took her to the community shop to purchase her favorite snacks.

We sat in the mini park not too far from the main road and chatted. It saddened me to tell her that I was leaving the island.

I knew that she had barely had anyone else to interact with in the community. Her mother deliberately shielded her from ridicules and it was understood.

We used a hard rock to sketch a hopscotch design on the asphalt. She enjoyed that game, though she struggled sometimes to land her left foot.

It was ok, I told her. Just have fun. No rules.

We played for about 30 minutes and sat down for a break. We ate the last of our snacks while we talked about whatever we wanted to.

After a while, I walked her back home. Before I left the gate, I promised her that I would keep in touch somehow, seeing that she could barely read manuscripts.

Hugging was not part of the Jamaican culture as a way of saying farewell, but pleasant smiles and good wishes were.

We smiled at each other, waved our hands, and I was off.

Halfway towards home, I looked back to have one last look at my cousin. I could see her wiping back tears from her eyes as I was. It was a sad moment.

CHAPTER 16: BIBLE STUDY AND PREPARING FOR DEPARTURE

It was mid-afternoon. I decided to prepare for Sunday evening Bible study. Ms. Manning was not sitting on the veranda when I got home. I figured that she, too, was preparing for Sunday evening service at the Anglican Church.

The housekeeper must have prepared something delicious because the aroma lingered on the veranda and throughout the home. I walked into the kitchen, greeted her, and glanced at the prepared meal. Steamed red snappers, potato salad, and vegetables were displayed in a most inviting way. Fresh, homemade carrot juice topped with nutmeg (one of my favorite spices), chilled in the drink holder on the countertop.

I was ready to eat. A quick wash of the hands and a speedy dash back to the kitchen must've startled the housekeeper, but her stern look did not allow her to flinch. I thanked her for preparing the meal and hoped that she would unfreeze her face and have dinner with me.

Ms. Manning's voice pleasantly interrupted my thoughts. "Hello, Winsome. How are you?" she politely asked.

"I am alright, Ms. Manning," I replied. "How are you?" I asked.

"Hungry," she replied with a chuckle.

"I am too!" I responded.

"Well, let's have dinner!" she said excitedly.

We prepared our meals and sat on the veranda. The veranda was the place where we relaxed and talked about whatever, as we watched the passersby. The view was not ideal because across the street was a house being built. Last year, we had a better view due to the lush grassy area and wild flowers.

That community was a scheme that contained about 40 homes 10-years prior. Now, it was a bustling area filled with large homes of the well-to-do. Some residents were retired, while others worked for the government or had their own businesses.

The Meyers, my cousins, lived diagonally from where I was, and they worked at Clarendon College, the school where I attended.

"This is absolutely delicious!" exclaimed Ms. Manning.

"Yes, it is," I agreed.

Steamed snapper fish was a well-known dish that most, if not all, Jamaicans fancied. Preparation is very important, along with how it's cooked. Apparently, the housekeeper was well embossed at her culinary skills. She was not very social or friendly, so there was no room to properly recognize her incredible effort.

Dinner had ended, and it was time to shower and attend Sunday evening service. Ms. Manning and I excused ourselves and began preparing for the services, respectively.

I showered, got dressed, collected my Bible, and headed out the door. It was a bit overcast, and I had hoped that it would not rain or that a kind person with transportation would give me a lift.

I continued walking, hoping to make it to church before it rained. I had an umbrella, but I left it at home, and I did not want to be late for church, so there was no going back home to get it.

The shoes on my feet had experienced an incredible amount of walking back and forth, and up and down the hill from church to school, and to town. My legs had developed strong muscles over the years as I footed it to almost everywhere that was within a 10-30 minute walk.

I wondered what it would be like in America when it came to transportation. I supposed that I would soon see for myself.

I was now about 2 minutes away from the church building. It had not rained, and I was thankful. It would not have been ideal to sit through the service clothed in wet attire.

As I entered the sanctuary, I noticed that everyone was kneeling down and praying. It was customary for one to pray before he joined the congregation for worship.

I found an empty space towards the center of the fellowship area, so I secured it to pray. Soon, I joined the singing service.

The main part of worshipping was through singing, so I looked forward to doing so. Songs were almost therapeutic, especially when they resonated or made a connection in my soul.

As I sang along with the congregation, I could not help feeling sad. Sad that it would have been the last service I had attended at that church where I was baptized.

It had not been long since I had become a member, but oh the things I experienced in such a time! The warmth of the 'mothers' of the church; the various functions that took place both at the church and away; the camaraderie amongst the members of compassion and kindness; the patience and long-suffering demonstrated by the young pastor and his office, and the list would seem endless if I continued.

I would certainly take fond memories with me wherever I went.

The teaching or Bible study had begun, and everyone was seated. I recalled the atmosphere feeling solemn, yet reassuring.

I had not experienced the presence of the Holy Spirit until later in my adult life. In retrospect, I had a similar feeling sitting there in the midst of the congregation. It was a tranquil, peaceful feeling, so much so that it seemed unreal.

I wanted to remain in that space or time.

The teaching was about God's love. I immediately recaptured John 3:16 in my thoughts.

I was curious to find out what kind of love it was that Jesus had for the world that caused God to send Him to die. I had not heard any sermon that truly defined that kind of love that made sense to me. One that resonated or shed clarity to the mind of a 19-year-old.

So, I set in my heart to discover this love and how to appreciate it properly.

It was 7:00 pm, and Bible study had ended. It was time to head back. Everyone was sifting out to their respective homes.

There was a group of women who were heading in my direction, so I took the liberty of joining them. On the way home, we chatted and laughed. We reminisced on the day and all that had transpired.

It was a good day.

Wednesday had arrived. Daddy planned to bring all the travel documents to me in preparation for Sunday's departure to America.

After working the night shift, he would get off work and then head to my place. I had not learned how to cook bashfully, but I wanted to prepare breakfast for us.

Daddy enjoyed authentic Jamaican dishes, including bird's peppers straight from the tree. On many occasions, he and I ate breakfast at the local breakfast joint located not too far from the marketplace in Chapelton.

His usual food was boiled bananas, yellow yams, callaloo, and liver. A cup of mint tea went well with the meal.

The waitresses knew us very well, so they brought out Daddy's bird peppers, red and whole.

I thought that it was a great idea to prepare the same, so off I went.

Because I knew my limitations, I boldly asked the housekeeper for a little help. She may have been antisocial, but she was an excellent cook. She agreed, and I was very thankful.

I knew how to peel the bananas and the yellow yams, so I did. I had difficulty slicing the yams into perfect circles, so I asked for help.

The water was at a rolling boil on the stove, so I added both the yams and bananas. A pinch of salt was added for taste.

It was time to cut up the callaloo. Freshly cut callaloo needs to be washed thoroughly to rid itself of any creepy crawlies that attack the leaves during growth, and I was afraid of them.

I politely asked the housekeeper if she could rinse it off, and she did.

I sliced up the tomatoes and onions to add to the chopped callaloo as added flavors while steaming it.

Next, it was time to prepare the livers. Beef liver had a certain way it was prepared, which was a bit technical for me, so I watched the housekeeper while she prepared and cooked it.

Next time, I will know how to.

Within an hour or so, breakfast was cooked.

CHAPTER 17: LEAVING HOME WITH FAITH AND FEAR

The kettle whistled while the water boiled to make the mint tea. The table was set as we awaited Daddy's arrival. Ms. Ruth and I sat on the veranda and chatted casually as we waited for Daddy to arrive. He normally rides his motorcycle, or someone may offer him a ride. It was almost 9:00 am when we heard the sound of a motorcycle approaching from around the bend. It was Daddy. He pulled up on the extra tiled area that was in front of the gate that led to the enclosed yard.

Today, he was wearing his police uniform. After work, he would shower, dress in civilian clothing, and go about his day or night. Without hesitation, I ran towards the entrance and held the gate open for him. We greeted each other with a smile and a slight nod. Ms. Manning stood up, greeted him warmly, and beckoned for him to enter the home. Daddy removed his police hat and shoes as the customs called for.

Afterwards, Ms. Manning gestured toward the kitchen, where he was greeted by the housekeeper, who was busy putting the final touches on the breakfast preparations. Both daddy and the housekeeper greeted each other, and we all thanked her for her efforts. It was time to eat. Ms. Manning prayed over the meal as we gathered at the table.

"Thank you for the breakfast invitation," said Daddy in his calm, reassuring voice. "I was supposed to work the morning shift today, but I switched with someone who had an emergency last night. I have a few other obligations with a court case later today, so I am wearing the uniform in preparation for it," he continued. Daddy's consideration of others was amazing. As far back as I could recall, he'd exercised such a respectful approach not only to adults, but to children as well. We were delighted to have him over for breakfast; yet, he was apologizing for inconveniencing us. Such was his character.

"Mr. Marshall, thank you for being courteous, but there is no need. It is our pleasure to have you join us for breakfast," Ms. Manning responded. Daddy nodded with gratitude.

"As you may guess, I am here to present the documents to you, Winsome, that you need for the trip. Take some time and look at everything carefully," he said.

"Yes, daddy, I will," I responded.

"Ms. Manning, since you have traveled internationally many times, would you mind looking over these documents with Winsome?" he asked. "If there is anything that needs to be corrected, we have a few days to do it," he continued."

Breakfast ended. Daddy, Ms. Manning, and I remained at the table after it was cleared. A large envelope was placed on the table by Daddy. From it, he pulled out my passport, plane ticket, contact information of his friend that I would connect with while in America, and some spending cash. He briefed us about them, then prepared to leave to run other errands.

We bade him farewell, while he and I confirmed that we would meet up with my mother on Friday in Chapelton. She wanted to bid me farewell before I left the island and shared something with me.

After Daddy left, Ms. Manning and I thoroughly looked at each document. No errors were found, so I secured it all in the large envelope and placed it in a secure place. I had some light chores to finish up, so I excused myself from the table and proceeded to work on them.

There was a small suitcase that I had stored in the corner of my room. I used it to transfer my clothing as I moved from one location to the other. It had a little dust on it from not being used for over two years, so I decided to dust it off and get it ready to use for the trip. I did not have much to pack, so the size was perfect.

Ms. Manning checked the weather in Florida on July 9. It was going to be hot, so I picked out an outfit that was conducive to the weather. One of the dresses that I wore to church would be perfect. A dressmaker who lived not too far away from me made it for graduation.

It was navy blue with short sleeves that came with a belt that fit perfectly. Knee-length rested appropriately and was befitting for a Christian according to the customary attire. Black low pumps went well with the little clutched purse that had been serving me for over five years.

I placed my outfit inside the free-standing closet that was inside the room. I wanted to have everything in place before the big day. Daddy was much disciplined in his line of duty. He would be prepared and ready ahead of time for his job, and I admired that.

I adopted that principle, so I gathered everything that I could have at least five days before the flight. One thing that I did not know how to do was how to stop panicking. I was a nervous wreck.

I was getting to go to a new place. A place where I had never been before. I would be gone from the environment and people that I had known to another world that I knew nothing about. I had heard many stories about it. Some were interesting, while others were scary.

I did not know what to expect, nor how to plan for it. I would be out of my comfort zone.

As I continued packing, I reflected on my siblings. I had not seen them in a while, though we lived not too far away. We all had split up after our mother migrated to Canada, and it was difficult knowing exactly where each of us was.

Communication was extremely limited during those times, unlike nowadays, where communication is only a touch of a key. Daddy was my go-to person for everything, including the whereabouts of my brothers and sister. He had not said anything to me about them, and I did not feel free enough to ask.

It was as though he had a lot on his plate because he was faced with the responsibility of the five of us since Mother was no longer on the island. I missed them terribly and hoped that we would see each other soon.

"Winsome, are you alright?" asked Ms. Manning from across the hall.

"Yes, I am," I responded.

"Carry on. I was just making sure that you are alright because you are so quiet, "she continued.

"I am preparing for the trip. Thanks for checking on me," I hollered back.

"I know. I will miss you," she said softly.

I could tell that Ms. Manning was beginning to miss me, and so was I. During breakfast, while she was helping me sort through the documents, her eyes began to tear up. Shortly after, I excused myself so that she could have some time to herself.

I would miss her terribly. She was like a mother to me.

I had packed enough and was a bit tired. It was almost 8:00 pm. After a shower, I read my Bible for a bit, then called it a night. The next day was Thursday, and I had planned to get my hair cornrowed.

One of the young women, Judith, who attended the same church as I, had promised to style my hair for the trip. We agreed on braids or cornrows to avoid the hassle of maintaining my hair.

The less bother the better at least that was my view. I wanted to avoid anything that would impede transitioning from one point to the other because I had heard that America was a fast-paced country.

CHAPTER 18: BRAIDS AND QUESTIONS OF FAITH

Judith lived about 5 minutes away from my house. After breakfast, I went to her house to get my hair braided. I took along some materials to read, including the mini Bible that remained so faithful over the years. I would be gone for at least three hours because I had long hair, and it would take a while to get it into small braids.

Judith and I saw each other from a distance and towards each other with wide smiles. She and I had a close relationship. We studied the scriptures together sometimes on Wednesday evenings before Bible study. We learned a lot together. I was going to miss her.

After a brief discussion, we agreed on a hairstyle and off she went. We chatted the whole time, reminiscing about the past two years. John 3:16 was still on my mind. I wanted to hear Judith's point of view about the scripture since she was a little older and had been baptized two years before I was.

"Judith, what do you think about John 3:16? Why would God give His only Son to die for the world?" I asked.

"I have the same question, Winsome. Maybe we should ask the mothers of the church or the pastor," she responded. "They should be able to answer it," she continued.

"I would really like to understand what kind of love that is. I would not want to give my only son to die for anything. I could not bear it," she said.

"I agree with you, Judith. That's why I am having a hard time processing it," I said.

"Are you planning to go to church on Sunday?" I asked.

"Of course!" exclaimed Judith. "I cannot afford to miss church services. It's forbidden in my eyes," she continued with a sarcastic chuckle.

For some odd reason, I felt the same. I was afraid to miss a church service. I did not know why. Condemnation probably? Afraid God would be upset with me? The church attendees that I became familiar with seemed to be strict about church attendance. I admired their dedication and aimed to follow suit.

After being baptized, I set my whole heart to be a devoted Christian. I did not know what exactly it meant to a devoted Christian, but I was willing to learn. That's what I thought, at least.

"Judith, are you going to ask the pastor about John 3:16 on Sunday?" I asked.

"I don't know. I don't think it's my place," replied Judith. "The pastor is untouchable. He is holy," she continued.

I did not have a response to Judith's last comment. I was a fairly newcomer and a novice. I was still in the learning stages, and I did not want anything to go wrong. Maybe we could ask the women, then, I thought to myself.

I did not know why I felt like we were on our own, but I did. I had never seen God, and I was afraid to ask for help because I did not want to lose my place. I decided to ask one of the women anyway, even if I would be stepping over my boundaries.

Judith was through cornrowing my hair. I thanked her and gave her the gift that I had brought for her.

For some reason, I felt like I had offended Judith when I asked her about talking with the pastor. She had gotten silent, and it was uncomfortable. I didn't really know what just happened, but I was concerned.

I did not know if she had experienced anything, and she did not want to talk about it, but I was not going to ask. I politely walked towards the gate, and I was on my way home.

I wanted to eat, showered and get in bed because tomorrow, Friday, I was scheduled to meet up with my mother and father. I had planned to hang out with Judith for a bit, but the atmosphere did not allow for a casual moment.

The daunting, sinking feeling of what just took place left an uneasy feeling in my belly. A flood of experiences bombarded my thoughts. Thoughts of my mother when she told me that she was afraid of God seeing her smoking. Thoughts of Daddy abandoning church attendance. Thoughts of Judith's reaction to talking with the pastor.

Why was there such a fear or stance to relating or relationship, I asked myself.

Thoughts of Judith's reaction to talking with the pastor. Why was there such a fear or stance to relating or relationship, I asked myself.

The culture that I was brought up in did not allow room for much grace or mercy. As a matter of fact, there was much condemnation not only from the environment as a whole, but especially from a religious standpoint.

I recalled a child being whipped or beaten with whatever the parent got hold of. Most of the time, the child was not beaten for being disrespectful. It was beaten for not cleaning the floor properly, or for breaking a dish, or not taking proper care of a younger sibling.

Sometimes the beatings were brutal and would leave permanent scars on the body. The culture did not allow room for error, a thing that was inevitable; yet, was severely punished for.

I recalled a boy being stoned by his mother. The child had misplaced something. The mother questioned him about it. He did not have a good enough explanation, so his mother picked up a couple of rocks that were close by and hauled them at him.

The child ran towards the back of the house to avoid being hit.

I also recalled a father beating his daughters for lying about a project that they were working on for him. He'd come home to check on the finished product and discovered a flaw. The father got hold of an electric cord and proceeded to whip the child. The child ended up with permanent scars.

Such was the culture. There was no room for mistakes.

As I reflected on my mother's approach to God about smoking, I wondered if she had adopted that view about a God who would not be gracious to her. The God that John 3:16 speaks of.

I had read numerous scriptures after my baptism that spoke of mercy, Matthew 5:7; about love, 1 Corinthians 13; and about kindness, Matthew 5:42.

Galatians 5:22-23 speaks of the fruits of the spirit, which were not being displayed amongst those who were admonishing others to.

As a new convert, I was confused. I witnessed the opposite of what the scriptures above admonished. I began to wonder if we were truly practicing what was being preached, or if we were doing our own things.

I began to examine my own journey, and I felt alone. I called it the journey within. I could not truly explain what was going on inside of me, but I wanted to find out.

It was as though I was on a mission. A mission that could take me anywhere at any time.

The desire had been in me since I had the dream when I was around 5 years old. The dream where I saw the name David written in red over a large, black hole or an endless black space.

I did not know where I would end up, but I had set my heart to saddle up for the ride.

It was Friday, and I was in Chapelton. Mother had plans to meet up at Daddy's work post so we could bid each other farewell for the trip that I was to take in a few days.

It was 9:00 am, and my mother had planned to meet us around 9:30. Daddy wasn't working at the courthouse today; instead, he was working at the bank as security, so I hung out with him while we waited for mother.

He and I chatted casually for a bit, and we even shared a cool thirst quencher. He was well-known in that small town.

It seemed as though every person who walked by exclaimed, Good Morning Mr. Marshall! He smiled and exchanged greetings with them.

He was not a person who craved the limelight, but the limelight seemed to find him. He responded with grace to it.

Mother arrived and daddy took a short break to mingle with us.

CHAPTER 19: CLOSURE BEFORE CROSSING OCEANS

There was a little shop just up the road, so we decided to hang out there for a bit. We spotted a table away from the traffic and secured it. Breakfast was still being served, so we ordered something to eat with a cup of the local favorite, mint tea.

Mother reached across the table, placed her hand on mine, and said, "Winsome, I will miss you." "I know that you have done all that your father asked of you, and I know that you will continue to," she continued. "I do not have much, but I would like to give you some spending cash," she said. She pulled out an envelope and gave it to me.

"Oh, thank you mommy. I will use it wisely," I said to her. "I know that you will," she responded. She took a hard pause and said this to my father, "Though I was not around for a long time, you have done what you could have to put Winsome through school. You have done well, and I am proud of her."

"I am too. Thank you," Daddy responded. It was time for Daddy to return to work, so he said goodbye and headed back.

Mother and I stayed and chatted for a bit. She sat across from me at the small rectangular table at the mom and pop eating joint. She reached out and held my hands and bore her heart out to me. I learnt that my father was the only love of her. It was never her intention to lose out on the marriage union that they shared.

As she spoke from her heart, she teared up from time to time. She reminisced about the first time that they met up to that point. It was clear to me that she was missing my father. She also apologized numerous times for not being a part of the children's journey as we grew up.

I did not know how to console her, but I reassured her that though she was not present physically, her financial support and phone calls meant a lot as we went through school. In those days, making a phone call to someone in a foreign country was tedious.

Placed in a high-traffic area in the middle of a major city was a free-standing phone booth. Every Sunday evening, people from all over the surrounding towns and communities formed one giant line. Each person took turns inserting coins in the drop box and calling their loved ones. One had to be prepared to spend all day to get a small opportunity to talk with their loved ones. That was how mother and we communicated over the years while she was in Canada. We looked forward to those moments.

"Mommy," I interrupted. "We don't look at it that way. We somehow knew that you did what was best for you and for us. You never abandoned us, and for that we are thankful," I reassured her.

She let out a sigh of relief and continued on. "Well, that makes me feel better," she said. "How do you feel about the trip to America? After all, you have never traveled before," she stated.

"The truth is, I do not know how to feel about it, mommy," I responded. "All I know to do is to trust daddy's plans," I said. "He has good intentions, it seems, so I believe that things will work out," I continued.

"You got baptized against my judgment, but I believe that you will be alright. Don't abandon church attendance as I did in my earlier days," she advised. "Your father said that he was not sure when you would return. I hope to see you again soon," she said.

"I hope so, too, mommy," I responded.

It was late in the afternoon. Mother and I shared quality time that was quite eye-opening and enjoyable. We said our goodbyes and went our separate ways.

As I began the walk back to my place, I replayed scenes of memories in my head of the 19 years I had spent on the island. I had hoped to see my siblings before I left. I did not know much about their whereabouts, and Daddy did not seem to want to discuss it.

One brother was living with my mother at her mother's place. We did not get a chance to interact much with each other when I went to visit my mother on the weekends. I did not know why he and I did not interact much, but it seemed normal. It was as though there was an understanding that we were not living the same lives, and I felt sorrow for him.

Much of Daddy's time and resources were invested in me more than any of the other children. I did not know why. I was labeled as daddy's "princess, pocketbook or even favorite child." I did not see myself as anything special to my father. All I knew was that I did not want to disappoint him.

I reflected on the river trips that my siblings and I took while we lived with our mother before she migrated to Canada. Those trips were bonding times, and I looked forward to them. The river was located within a 10-15 minute walk just below the foot of the hill from our house.

On Saturdays, mother had us load up the clothes bins because it was time to wash the clothes in the river water. Such were the customs in those days. As we journeyed down the steep hill to the river bed, we would stop and pick mangoes from the mango trees or whatever fruits that we could get our hands on. That's how lunch was provided.

When we arrived at the riverbed, the females unloaded the

clothing and proceeded to wash while the boys went for a dive. There was a huge rock that projected out of the water that my brothers found pleasure in jumping off into the water. I was afraid of the deep, so I never ventured close to it.

My brothers would sometimes climb to the pinnacle of the rock and jump 20 feet or so into the water. They were young and fearless. Mother, my sister, and I washed and beat clothes in the water and on the rocks until we were exhausted. We then spread them on tree limbs or rocks to dry in the sun.

There were no modern-day washers and dryers, so we made use of what we had and learned to be thankful. Sunny days on Saturdays were most welcome, though the sun beamed its wrath on us. It was needed; nevertheless, to dry the clothing so that we would have a fresh set of clothes for school or whatever else.

We would often spend the entire day at the river just hanging out and having a great time. I enjoyed those days.

I made it home. Ms. Manning was sitting on the veranda looking at the passersby while waving at them.

"Good evening, Ms. Manning," I said. "Oh, good evening, Winsome," she responded. "How was the meeting with your mother?" she asked. "It went well. I will miss her," I responded. "I know. It's expected," she responded in a most assuring tone.

"Well, it was a long day, so I am going to settle in for the evening," I said. "Three more days! How are you feeling about all of this?" she pressed. "Yes, three more days. I really don't know how to feel. I am trying to embrace the potential change," I responded. "Fair enough," replied Ms. Manning in a most polite gesture.

I chuckled, then went to my room. I was not hungry, so I did not bother to eat. I was getting anxious, I supposed, after Ms. Manning reminded me that the trip was in three days.

It was a good day, I thought. There was closure after the conversation with my mother. I jumped in the shower, then brushed my teeth. I was a bit tired, so I called it a night.

I spent the next three days at home. Everything was washed and packed for the trip. I had saved some coins in a jar when I resided with my aunt, but after I left her place, they were nowhere to be found. It saddened me because I saved a part of my lunch money many times because I wanted to see how much would have been saved had I continued adding coins.

Oh well, life goes on, I thought.

CHAPTER 20: MY LAST GOODBYE AND FIRST FLIGHT

Monday night was the last night on the island before I flew out. Daddy had stopped by on Monday afternoon to bid me goodbye since the college had planned to bus us all to the airport the following day. He gave me a pep talk while sitting on the enclosed veranda. All of the instructions that I should follow from that point until I reached his friend in America were neatly placed in an accessible envelope. I was not going to disappoint him.

It was an early morning flight, so Daddy decided to leave a bit early so that I could get a good night's rest. He was not a hugger, so when he hugged me, it felt strange and surreal. If only I had known that it would have been the last time that I would have seen my father. He passed away suddenly after I had migrated to America.

It was Tuesday morning on July 9. I was very anxious, which caused me to be restless, so I did not sleep much. Ms. Manning must have noticed the light on in my room, so she knocked on the door and asked if she could enter. We chatted until it was time for me to get dressed to get on the bus.

We reminisced about the last two years. We laughed and cried and laughed and cried again. I was really going to miss such a kind and generous person. She was one of a kind.

The bus arrived. Ms. Manning and I bade each other farewell. I collected my belongings and proceeded to the bus. It was filled with other students and college staff members. We all greeted each other with excitement and well-wishes.

I sat beside my cousin, who attended a different school, but was on her way to America as well. She lived in another town, so we did not see each other as often. The driver was now enroute to the airport after someone prayed over the trip.

My cousin and I were excited to sit together so we could chat all the way to the airport, which was a little over an hour away. She had attended Edwin Allen High School, while I attended Clarendon College, but we made attempts to keep in touch throughout the years. She had a bubbly personality, while I was a bit of an introvert.

We chatted about everything, it seemed including the visit to Disney World in Orlando, Florida. She and I had never gone to Disney World, but the travellers were briefed about it. We had heard that it was a "world" within a "world." She and I could not wait to see such a massive place!

We broke out in silly giggles as the bus dodged pot holes on the country road. "Is this your first time on an airplane, Winsome?" she asked. "Yes, it will be," I replied. "I am nervous, though," I continued. "How about you?" I asked. "I am nervous, too," she replied. "This is my first time traveling as well," she said.

The bus arrived at that airport, and it was time to unload and check in. After clearing security, we all gathered at the boarding gate and awaited our flight.

Daddy had gotten in contact with the group's leader after we arrived at the airport. He was concerned about the trip and how I would fare. Nevertheless, he assured me that I was going to be alright. It was good to hear that he checked on me. I entrusted my well-being to him wholeheartedly.

Air Jamaica flight "XYZ" was announced. "That's our flight!" exclaimed the group's leader. She had an aura about her that exuded confidence and assurance. As a director of students' affairs at Clarendon College, her approach to the role both on and off campus paralleled the whittiness by which she operated the trip.

Each of us followed her directive as we boarded the flight.

My cousin and I sat next to each other, and we were super excited because we wanted to continue our conversation about the American experience. After waiting for about 30 minutes, the pilot announced take-off in 10 minutes. The seatbelt signs were turned on as we awaited takeoff.

I closed my eyes and prayed silently. My cousin did not seem to mind. She was a giggler, but remained quiet while I took a moment of silence. The aircraft began moving slowly, then faster, and we were suddenly in the air!

We both began laughing with fear and excitement, simultaneously. It was our first time flying in an aircraft, and it was an amazing experience in the air and above the clouds.

As I looked at the space outside the window, my thoughts began to drift on God, the Creator of what I was witnessing, far above the earth. The clouds, space, sun, and the massive expanse in mid-air. A sense of gratefulness enveloped my being. Humility and sheer reverence gripped me as though they were saying "respect" is due to their creator.

The oneness that I felt with Him took me back to the dream that I had at age five about the large jet black space with the name David written in it. I did not understand what it really was that I was experiencing in midair. All I knew was that something was happening that caused me to honor and respect Him even more.

"Winsome. Hey, Winsome!" yelled my cousin. "Hey," I said. "How long were you calling me?" I asked her. "I called your name five times," she said. "I am sorry. My thoughts were somewhere else," I responded.

She and I began chit-chatting about our whereabouts in America after the trip to Disney World. She was going to visit her family in Florida, who lived about 45 minutes from Disney World, then return to Jamaica. She was a bit younger than I and was still attending school in Jamaica. Her parents, like my father, had allowed her to take a summer trip to America.

She and I had agreed to room together at the hotel while we visited Disney World. Our conversation was interrupted by the pilot, who announced that we would be landing in Orlando, Florida, in 30 minutes.

The time flew by while my cousin and I communicated. I felt a nervous tingle shoot through my belly in anticipation. I did not know what to expect. I had heard much about such a great country, and was anxious to see it for myself.

It was an early flight, so the skyline's magnificent glory shone in all its beauty from the sun's rays onto the beautifully designed man-made structures that were visible as the aircraft lowered to a landing. The captivating layout of the massive structures was absolutely breathtaking. I guess what I had heard was not too far from what I was seeing.

I felt a hard hit on my arm, then I heard my cousin yell, "Look, look, Winsome! We are in America!" "It is so big! Look at the humongous buildings!" she yelled. "They are massive, yes!" I exclaimed.

As the aircraft halted for a landing, reality set in. I felt like a fish out of water. All of a sudden, I felt a sense of loneliness as though I was alone. I was missing Jamaica, especially my father. I really wanted him to know that we had landed.

The seatbelt signs were turned off. The stewardess announced that we could deplane. The voice of the group's leader directed us to wait outside the waiting area until all the group members had deplaned.

It felt surreal. The air felt cool and mild. The complete opposite of the tremendous tropical heat that I was used to. Thirty minutes or so had passed, and we were all gathered in one spot. The leader had arranged for transportation to take us all to a hotel in close proximity to the venue.

CHAPTER 21: AMERICA A WORLD WITHIN A WORLD

The ride from the airport to the hotel was pleasant. The roads were busy. Highways and bypasses seemed spectacular...kind of like in the American movies that I had watched at times while I was in Jamaica. Everything seemed to be in abundance and larger than I could imagine. It was indeed a whole new world within a world.

My cousin and I sat together. We commented on almost everything that we saw all the way to the hotel. There was so much to see and talk about. We came to a halt and were directed by the driver of the bus to the entrance of the hotel.

It was the middle of summer, but the air conditioning system at the hotel felt like winter. It was cold inside. My cousin and I snuggled up to each other as we followed the leader of the group. While she checked us all into the hotel to secure our rooms, we all waited in the lobby and chatted for a bit amongst ourselves.

We all agreed on one thing, and that was that what we heard about America was true. It's a beautiful country with friendly, courteous people. At least what we had experienced so far. The leader gave us all a room key, and we all headed to our rooms, respectively.

After we got settled in and showered, it was time to have dinner. The evening was still young, so we all went to a local Jamaican restaurant that was within walking distance. During the walk, we were all captivated by the enormous skyscrapers all around. The streets were nicely paved with visible pedestrian crossings that were most welcoming.

We appreciated the courtesy that was extended to us by the commuters as we walked along the busy highways on our way to the restaurant. Orlando, Florida, reminded us of Jamaica with its warm, tropical climate.

As we entered the restaurant, we were greeted with the most friendly, warm greetings by the attendees. As they escorted us to our seats, they did so with a smile. They went out of their way, it seemed to make us feel welcome.

We spent the next 1.50 hours eating and having a good time. It was time for us to head back to the hotel to prepare for the Disney World tour the following day. It was a 15-minute drive from the hotel.

The day had arrived, and we were off to visit this grand place that we had heard so much about while in Jamaica. The structural view from the hotel to Disney World was breathtaking. Engineering took on a whole other form as we observed the massive skyscrapers that lined the busy streets of Orlando.

The winding bypasses looked like artwork at its best. There was no way we could have missed our destination, seeing how precise the overhead interstate directions were on such beautifully asphalted streets.

Walt Disney World was now in view. Everyone gasped with gaping jaws as we all laid our eyes on such enormous structures. Disney World was indeed a "world." It bore its name befittingly. The castle-like design of one of the art pieces was beyond description. We could not wait to go inside and experience what we were all there for.

Ten minutes into the guided tour, the only word that I could use to describe the interior was heavenly. I have not gone to heaven, but I read about the street that was paved with gold in the Bible, and someone must've gleaned into heaven, because the architectural design was certainly nothing short of it.

The five-hour experience was certainly worth the trip. It was time for us to head back to the hotel. We spent the next several days there, where we got the coveted opportunity to experience America a little bit more before dispersing to our respective places until it was time to return to Jamaica.

Daddy had already made prior arrangements for me to connect up with his dear friend in Florida, who would reveal to me whatever plans Daddy had for me while in the USA. I did not know what the plans were, but I was poised to continue obeying my father's plans. His friend was to meet me at the hotel in three days. He would share the plans with me, then.

All communications were between him and my father, and my job was to follow the plan. Over the next few days, my cousin and I spent our time talking about our whereabouts. She was going to visit her aunt, who lived in Ft. Lauderdale, which was not too far from Orlando.

I, on the other hand, did not know where I was going to end up, or where exactly in Florida, Daddy's friend lived. My cousin and I promised to keep in touch somehow, though we did not know exactly how, since we did not know for sure where we would end up.

The day had arrived for me to leave the hotel. I was advised by the group's leader to wait in the lobby until I was picked up. The description and name of my father's friend were given to me by Daddy, so I had an idea of who would pick me up.

Twenty minutes had passed, and a tall gentleman walked up to me. He seemed to know exactly who I was because he introduced himself and told me things that only Daddy could have said to him.

He told me that I was going to stay with him and his wife for a while, and that he would explain everything to me once he got home. He also lived in Ft Lauderdale, where my cousin was going to visit her aunt in a few days.

Twenty minutes later, we arrived at my father's friend's house. I was greeted by his lovely wife, who showed me to my room. I felt at home, but I was missing my father and the life that I was used to in my country.

There was a subtle feeling in my gut that told me that I was not going to return home with the college crew. "Winsome, are you hungry?" My dad's friend asked me. "No, I am not," I replied. "Well, dinner is prepared when you are ready to eat," he continued. "Thank you," I replied.

I went to my room and began unpacking my suitcase. My dad's friend had already told me that he would enlighten me the following day about my fate. While I was unpacking, my thoughts began to drift.

I wondered what the conversation was going to be about. I wondered what Daddy was up to. I did not have the luxury of contacting him, so I relied on his friend to relay messages from him to me.

I also wondered where my future was going from that point on. I had already graduated, so the next phase of my life should be taking place any moment, I was thinking.

The day had passed, so I took a shower, said good night to my dad's friend and his wife, and I went to bed. I was hungry, but I did not feel comfortable eating. Maybe it was because I was in a new environment. Or, maybe I was a bit frightened about the unknown.

The next day arrived. Breakfast was prepared, and I was asked to join the family at the breakfast table.

While we were having breakfast, he said, "Winsome, I realize that you may be wondering why you are here with us, and not with those that you arrived here from Jamaica."

"Your father asked me to do a big favor for him that I want to talk about with you," he continued.

Upon hearing those words, my stomach was in a knot. Maybe it was intuition, or discernment, I could not tell. All I knew was that something felt uncomfortable in my gut.

"What do you mean, sir?" I asked. "Your father wants me to arrange a marriage for you so that you can become a U.S. citizen," he said.

After hearing those words, I was dumbfounded. I had not heard of that kind of arrangement before. Maybe it was because I was sheltered and was not exposed to much, and also because of my age. I was only 19-years-old.

I began processing in my mind what was just said. It changed my whole outlook and expectations of where my future plans were heading. I had not even thought about marriage or anything close to it.

On the contrary, I was thinking about going to a university, graduating, and then getting married and starting a family. That vision would have been accomplished around age 25, I was projecting, not 19, and without a 4-year degree.

"Oh, wow," I responded. "I was not expecting to hear something like this," I continued. "However, I will obey what Daddy has asked you to do for me," I said.

CHAPTER 22: AN ARRANGEMENT I COULD NOT REFUSE

After hearing the news, I wanted to have a conversation with my father. There were so many questions that I wanted to ask him, but I knew not to. The culture would not allow me to question my parents, especially when they were still responsible for my well-being.

After my mother returned from her lengthy stay in Canada, she was more approachable. I could talk with her. I suppose that she was enlightened by the Canadian culture where teenagers conversed with their parents candidly. I knew, however, that mother would have directed me back to my father, which would have been proper since he was the governing parent.

"Thank you for letting me know. I would like to be excused from the table, please," I said to my dad's friend and his wife. "Of course," they replied.

I had to get to a quiet place to reflect on what I had just heard, so the bedroom became my solace. All of a sudden, I was restless. It was as though I was wrestling within myself. Strange. Praying was inevitable. The only being that I could turn to at that moment was the Lord.

I had not learned how to pray for specific things or how to listen for the Holy Spirit, but the restlessness within me was overwhelming.

Before I went to the bedroom, my dad's friend said, "By the way, Winsome, we are relocating to Alabama. My wife was offered a job there, so we will be leaving in a few days." "Oh, alright. Thanks for the information," I responded.

Off I went to the bedroom. I closed the door behind me, then I lay on the bed. My mind was racing. I wondered if something was going on with my father, why he made such a life-changing decision for me. I wondered if he was planning to relocate to the US and wanted to ensure that I was going to be there permanently. I wondered if he was not well and did not want me to know. I wondered....

I could not wait until daylight. I wanted to talk with my father's friend about the unsettling arrangements, so I got up early the following morning. He was getting ready for work. I wanted to have a conversation with him before he left, so I hurried to the kitchen where he was preparing a cup of tea.

"Good morning," I said. "Hi. Are you ok?" he asked. "Actually, I am not. May I ask you a question, please?" I asked him. "Of course," he responded. "Did daddy tell you why he has asked you to arrange a marriage for me?" I asked. "No, he did not. He is my dear friend, and I trust him. I know that he has good intentions for you," he elaborated. "You will be alright. I gave him my word," he continued.

I nodded my head in acknowledgement and went back to the room. The silence was deafening. My heart was troubled, and I did not know why. It reminded me of the feeling that I had while I was back home after I got baptized. An unsettling feeling in my belly.

It was as though there were two authorities or forces wrestling in my soul, and each wanted to dominate the other. I got down on my knees and began to pray. I asked the Lord to give me His peace and to reveal what was happening.

The day had arrived for us to leave Florida for Alabama. The distance between the two adjoining states was about 8 hours. We got up early and headed out. The scenic, country view was calming and certainly needed.

My father's friend and his wife conversed quite a bit during the trip. I remained fairly quiet for most of the drive, which was alright with me, since I was still adapting to the surroundings.

Though I was in Florida for a short while, I was going to miss it because it reminded me so much of Jamaica with its tropical weather and bright colors. Exotic fruit trees and vegetation could be seen along the coast and in private homes. Daffodils and sunflowers graced the land lines as though showing off their glorious beauty for all to see.

Passersby and neighbors with native dialect were comforting...providing a homely vibe that riveted assurance.

We crossed over the state line and were now in Alabama. The sign "Welcome to Alabama the Beautiful" was in bold writing on a green background street sign logo. It was indeed a beautiful state with the most agricultural land that I had ever laid eyes on.

Farm animals of various kinds, such as sheep, cows, and horses, graced the rolling prairies with their lush green grass and beautiful farm land. It was a vivid reminder of Daddy's farm land in Jamaica, which brought back precious memories of the numerous trips that Daddy, I, and other family members took there.

Oh, how I began missing Jamaica!

For a while, I captured the beauty of a small part of such a grand country. The news that I had heard a few days ago was settling in me. I came to grips with the reality of what I was going to do, but my spirit was still unsettled.

It was about 7:00 pm when we arrived. We pulled up at a mid-sized family home on the outskirts of the city, where we were going to reside for a while. Everyone was tired from the trip, so we unpacked and grabbed something light to eat for supper and decided to settle in for the night.

The next day, the family had planned to get out and tour the city in order to become familiar with a few main places until we learned our way around. My first priority was finding a church to attend.

We rode through the city, where we discovered numerous restaurants, churches, and organizations such as informational centers for incoming residents. We stopped in and picked up a few brochures that could help us in navigating the city. The brochures were very informative.

In it, we located recreational centers, landmarks, and everything necessary, hubs that could help us settle into a city of about 70,000 residents.

Before we headed back home, we stopped at a local fried chicken chain restaurant where we ate some delicious fried chicken and okra. I had never had fried okra before. They were yummy.

On the way home, I plucked out the brochure from my jacket pocket. I wanted to find a church that was in close proximity to where the house was. I noticed that there was one within a 20 minute-walk from the residence.

I did not mind walking to worship on Sundays, but I also noticed that rarely anyone walked in that community. As a matter of fact, I barely saw anyone walking on the streets while we were riding around the town.

Additionally, it was made known to me that there was no available public transportation, subways, or passenger trains anywhere in the city or close by. Commuters relied on private vehicles or taxi services.

I had not learned how to drive, and even if I did, I could not afford to purchase a vehicle. Taxi services were expensive, and I had not worked before. Suddenly, I had to "grow" up. Daddy was not around anymore to foot the responsibilities, and I must survive.

After settling in for over two weeks, we had become friendly with our neighbors. I inquired about a closer place to worship. Someone told me about a married couple who held church services in their home. As a matter of fact, she had gone to visit one Sunday and was quite pleased with the sermon.

After hearing such good news, I informed my neighbor that I would like to attend the service that upcoming Sunday. She seemed excited and promised that she would go with me. I was excited as well.

CHAPTER 23: THE PATIO CONVERSATION THAT CHANGED MY PATH

Sunday morning arrived. I got dressed and waited for the neighbor to come over. I stood on the porch so that I could see her as she entered the driveway. She was spotted a little ways off, so I walked toward her.

She had a vehicle, but decided to walk since the residential church home was located in the neighborhood. "Good morning," she said. "Good morning to you as well. Thank you for taking the time to go to church with me," I responded. "No problem. It's been a while since I attended, so I am looking forward to it," she replied. "Let's go," she said.

We began walking. Within 8 or so minutes, we arrived at the residence. Several cars were parked in the driveway. We walked up to the front door, and someone beckoned us to enter. We were greeted and introduced to the owners and their children, along with the guests.

They directed us to the seating area where my neighbor and I sat side by side. Shortly after, the owner stood up and took his place at the podium. He made an official introduction of himself, prayed, and delivered the sermon.

After the sermon, he met with each person, where he had a brief conversation about each person's whereabouts and church homes. It was now time for dismissal, and we each went our separate ways.

It was a good day. On our way home, my neighbor and I conversed about the sermon. We enjoyed the service and were pleased to meet new people. We agreed to visit again soon. We said goodbye to each other and parted ways.

At home, my dad's friend's wife had prepared dinner. We sat together at the dinner table, ate, and had a good conversation about the day. During the conversation, he mentioned that he wanted to talk with me about something, but that it would be the following day after he got off work.

I said alright and continued with dinner. The day had passed, so shortly afterwards I excused myself to shower and got in bed.

While in bed, I began thinking of what he wanted to talk about. I was not sure how I would handle hearing something else that would put my mind in a state of confusion. I had not spoken to my father except through his friend.

I decided to contact him somehow. Access to international phone conversations was limited. There was a home phone, but the hassle of connection was discouraging. I had to make contact somehow, so I decided to send a letter to my father.

It would have taken a few weeks before the letter arrived, and the same for a response.

The following day, my dad's friend got home earlier than his usual schedule. I was sitting in the living room, casually talking with his wife. "Hi. How are you all?" he asked. "Ok. We responded." "How was your day?" his wife asked. "It was alright. Didn't have much production today. We have to wait for another load of peanuts to arrive," he continued.

He worked at a local factory that produced products such as cooking oil and peanut products. He landed that job when we all relocated from Florida.

"Winsome, do you have a minute?" he asked. "Of course," I responded. "I would like to talk with you on the patio," he responded.

I excused myself from the living room and joined him on the patio. "Do you remember when I told you that your father asked me to arrange for someone to marry you?" he asked. "Yes, I remember," I responded. "Well, I think that I found someone that your father would approve of," he said.

He told me his name that I will call T. He went on to say nothing but great things about T and the kind of person that he was. From the sound of it, that man would have been approved by Daddy had he met him. He would have passed the test reputational, family status, and financially.

It was arranged for him and me to meet the following weekend. It has been a week since the letter was sent to my father. A letter that asked Daddy so many questions about the arranged marriage.

I was hoping that he did not view the questions that were asked in the letter as me being disrespectful, since it was uncultured to question one's parents about matters if they assumed the role of financial and economic responsibilities for an offspring.

"Oh?" I responded, questioning my own thoughts that this was really happening. That this was real. I was really going to marry someone whom he or I did not know.

I wondered about his thoughts, how his family would take the news, how it would all play out. I was curious about his beliefs, age preferences, goals, and so much more!

"I don't know how to respond to this, sir, truthfully," I replied. "I realize that you are doing my father a favor, but I do not know how to process all of this," I continued.

"I understand, Winsome," he acknowledged. "These kinds of arrangements happen quite often, so it's going to be ok," he consoled.

"When and where are we supposed to meet?" I asked. "This coming Sunday at 4:00 pm," he responded. "It will be here at the house. You all will talk privately on the patio," he continued.

I had a couple of days to prepare for the meeting. I was hoping that the letter had arrived early to Daddy so that he could reconsider and allow me to return home.

After all, he had everything in place for continued education and even a secured position once I graduated from university. The kind of job that he had allowed him to "rub elbows" with people that an average worker would not have been privy to.

I had always known that Daddy's intentions for my well-being were good; I just could not wrap my mind around such a decision that he had made. It was not making sense, and I needed clarity.

It was as though for the first time, I wanted to resist his decision for my life. The battle inside of me felt like the one I had after I got baptized. It was fighting for something bigger than myself.

Sunday arrived. I had been waiting on the porch for about 15 minutes when I saw a car pull in the driveway. A tall fellow opened the car door, closed it behind him, and began approaching the house.

"Hello," he greeted. "Oh, hi," I responded. "You must be Winsome?" he asked. "Yes, I am," I responded.

My dad's friend had already told me his name, so I greeted him as such. "You may come inside," I said while I directed him towards the foyer.

My father's friend and his wife greeted him as he and I headed towards the patio. I offered him something to drink as the customs were for one's guests.

We sat across from each other as we prepped ourselves to have a conversation. "How do you guys know each other?" I asked. "Do you mean, R?" "Yes, R," I responded. (R was the initial of my father's friend's first name, so T addressed him as such). "I am his supervisor," he responded. "Oh, I see," I responded. "He told me that he and your father had been knowing each other for some time, and that they are like brothers," he continued. "I suppose. My father said the same thing to me," I responded.

CHAPTER 24: MY TROUBLED HEART

As we continued our conversation, many things were discovered. He was the only son of two children for his parents. He had a sister. He was the "apple" of his mother's eye and had a grandmother who thought the world of him. He stated that he lived a life that made his parents very proud.

I asked him about the proposal that R had made to him as it pertained to him and me. He told me that he had heard of marriage arrangements before, but he did not know much about them. I did not either.

I also asked him what his thoughts were as it pertained to him and me. He said that after meeting me, that was something that he would do. I was especially surprised that he was an American and had not engaged in such an arrangement before; yet, he wanted to.

His mother whipped across my mind. I had not met her, but for some reason, I began feeling a sense of guilt. The restlessness came back. It was as though I was embarking on something that was unchristian like, but I was unsure.

I expressed to him that I was uncomfortable about the idea and that I was unsure of what the decision would be until I heard from my father. He understood, based on his response.

We were both very young, 19 and 20, respectively. Neither of us knew anything about relationships, really, or much less marriage. He had not gotten advice from anyone, it appeared, so everything became uncertain.

We agreed to meet again in two weeks. The hope was that we both had more clarity about such a decision, and I would have gotten a response from my father, hopefully. We ended our conversation and bade each other farewell until we saw each other again.

My father's friend R wanted to know how the meeting went after T left. I told him the truth. Neither of us knew anything about such a proposal, and we agreed to meet again. He said alright, and agreed.

It was comforting to see that he agreed because engaging in such a move would affect everything as we knew it to be.

Two weeks had passed, and I had not received a response from my father. I wondered if the mail had gotten lost or if it was delayed. T was on his way, and I was not prepared to make any decisions. Not without hearing from my father, I thought.

I conversed with R and expressed to him that I was not prepared. He encouraged me to go through with it, because Daddy would have agreed.

The doorbell rang. It was T. I greeted him and beckoned for him to enter. After greeting the others, we proceeded to the patio. "Winsome, it's good to see you again," he proceeded. "It's good seeing you as well, T," I responded. "Well, what are your thoughts about marriage?" I asked. "I want to go for it," he responded. "You do?" I asked. "Of course," he said, surprisingly. "Do your family members know about this decision?" I asked. "At least your mother?" I continued. "No. No one knows," he responded.

My heart dropped in my chest. I excused myself and beckoned for R to join T and me. I wanted to bring him into the conversation. We told him about our decision to get married. He was relieved, it appeared.

Immediately, he arranged for a private 4-party vows that would take place in the coming weeks. T agreed, and so did I.

The day for the exchange of vows arrived. R, T, and another witness gathered in front of the clergy. As the vows were exchanged, I thought about my father and the rest of my life's journey.

The uneasy feeling inside my gut troubled me. It felt like I had broken a law, a covenant, or something. I could not articulate it. I looked at T's facial expression while he repeated the vows; it expressed joy and uncertainty, simultaneously. Crazy.

"You are now husband and wife," said the preacher. Those words resounded in my head in a troubling fashion. We walked out of the venue without saying a word to each other.

I looked at my dad's friend. The look on his face reverberated accomplishment of sorts. He had done what his best friend had asked of him, and he had done it well, in my estimation.

Immediately after we were wedded, T and I went to a place he had prepared for us. I immediately saw that he was ready for married life, at least in material things.

He had chosen a top-of-the-line housing, the latest model vehicle, and the freedom for me to make our house a home. I was impressed with his efforts.

I played the part of a wife, at least what I could have with what I had. We knew absolutely nothing about married life. Everything seemed so discreet and secretive that even if we could have gotten advice from someone, we were both too young and immature to ask.

After a short while of trying to make the best of what was allotted to us, I made a decision. That decision took every ounce of boldness and faith (as I knew it) to accomplish.

A little over a year had passed since we eloped. During that time, I wrestled within. There was no rest or peace. It was as though there was a fierce war taking place inside of me, and it was tearing me apart.

I tried to ignore it. It was the same feeling that I had after I had gotten baptized. The war had begun. That was the only way that I could make my mind understand my plight.

Prayer was now my daily meal. As I read the New Testament scriptures, marriage and the connection between Christ and the church stuck out. It was as though something hit me in my chest when I read that scripture.

I had not known what condemnation felt like, but whatever it was, I was experiencing it. It was the worst pain I had ever endured.

It was as though God Himself was saying, "You have taken what was meant for good, for usage," I thought. Oh, the feeling was unbearable!

I could not continue with what I had committed to, though my beloved father arranged it with great intentions. I must tell T what was happening to me, I thought. But how? If it were up to him, he would have weathered it out.

What I am going to say to Daddy, I wondered. The pressure was becoming undeniably crucial. I had to get in touch with Daddy somehow, I thought.

Until this day, I cannot say how I got hold of my father, but I did. Nervousness, fear, and guilt rested on me as I sat on the other end of the telephone, preparing to tell my father that I was going to break a covenant with him for my true father.

It's a tremendous feeling that I still cannot articulate.

As daddy listened on the other end, I proceeded to say, good evening, daddy. "Hello, Winsome. How are you?" he replied. "I do not know, Daddy. I have been trying to get in touch with you since I arrived in America," I responded. "I realize that. I got your letter," he replied. "Oh. Well, I had not heard back from you," I said. "I know. I wanted you to spread your wings and fly," he replied. "You must come into your own. I have taken you as far as I could. You have everything in you to do well in life," he continued.

I had never cried to my father before, but I could not help tearing up. His words solidified what I had known all along. "Daddy, I cannot continue in this arranged marriage," I confessed. "I read in the Bible that the way that I got married was not how God wanted me to," I continued. "God reigns supreme," he said. "I am not God. If you are troubled by the arrangement, do not forget that you will always have a room here," he consoled me.

After hearing those words, I broke down again into tears. The guilt that I had about disappointing my father was suddenly no longer in my belly. It was as though God Himself had freed me.

Daddy's words were so comforting and assuring that I felt like I could fly. My spirit was free! "Daddy, I did not want to tell you about my dilemma because I did not want to disappoint you," I said. "Winsome, you are my daughter. I could not have asked anything more of you," he said. "There is nothing that you can do that would cause me to be disappointed because you would have done so already," he said. "Thank you daddy for everything," I said.

After the conversation ended between my father and me, I pondered over what was said. I did not say anything to anyone, not even T. I had to process every word so that I could make a proper life-changing decision.

The next day arrived. I must have a conversation with T, I decided.

CHAPTER 25: BREAKING FREE THROUGH FAITH AND CONVICTION

He and I had eaten breakfast. We sat staring in space as though he had an inclination that something was up. I could feel the uneasiness in the atmosphere.

"T, there is something that I want to talk with you about," I broke the silence and said. "I have a suspicion," he replied. "How so?" I asked. "I can tell that you have been wrestling with something for a while now," he continued. "As a matter of fact, I am," I replied. "I cannot continue with the marriage," I said. "I should not have entered it from the very beginning, but I was too afraid to disappoint my father," I continued.

"My mother was disappointed as well because she wanted to be a part of everything, so I understand," he said. "Oh, wow," I responded. "I am sorry for putting you and your family through this," I apologized. "It's ok. They will understand," he said.

The following day, I called my dad's friend, R, and explained everything to him. He was surprised, but there was nothing that he could have done about it. My mind was made up.

Alabama was a state where I had no family members. There was no support except for Daddy's friend, and he had his own family and life to tend to. The decision that I had made to leave the marriage was one of faith.

I had come to have a little understanding of faith while I was struggling with the decision. I had come to understand that faith was an action word, and I had to literally do something about the marriage.

With the little understanding that I had about a good conscience before the Lord, was about to be tested. "Lord, I am sorry for using what's meant for good for my own benefit," I immaturely confessed to God. "I want to be married, but not like this. The next time that I get married, it will be proper," I prayed.

It was as though I was making a promise or a one-sided covenant with God. Shortly after, the marriage ended.

I did not know where to go; all I knew was that I had to trust the voice or conviction that rested heavily on me. I was on my own.

God had blessed me with a job, a place to live, and a vehicle to drive. They were menial, but I was very grateful.

I continued attending the at-home church until the pastor prophesied something to me that caused me to leave the setting, permanently.

After attending church service one Sunday, I went home and was pondering over the sermon and what was prophesied over me by the pastor. The pastor had a son who was older than I, whom he wanted me to marry.

I was not ready for marriage, so I politely said no. He placed his hand on my head and prophesied that God told him that I would be his son's wife.

I was still immature in spiritual things and had not experienced the voice of God. Also, I did not want to disobey God either, so I did not know what to do.

After my divorce, I promised myself and God that I would marry for the right reasons, but at that point, I was not ready for another marriage.

That night, I had a dream. In the dream, I was lying in bed. To my left, there was a giant being, dressed in white. In his hand was a Bible. He opened it to the book of Jeremiah and gave it to me.

The scripture that he gave was Jeremiah 14 verse 14: The prophets prophesy lies in my name: I sent them not, neither spake unto them: they prophesy unto you a false vision and divination, and a thing of nought, and the deceit of their heart. (King James Version).

The giant being prompted me to show the scripture to the pastor. I was sore afraid! I did not want to show such a scripture to a man of God, I thought to myself. I became restless.

The following Wednesday night was bible study. I needed to talk to someone about the dream before I went to bible study. The pastor's son and I had a respectful relationship, so I decided to reveal the dream to him.

I told him about the experience, including the prompting to show the scripture to his father. I also let him know that I was afraid to. His response was, "Winsome, if God told you to do it, you must obey."

At that point, I decided to show his father the scripture on Wednesday after bible study.

As I walked to Bible study that Wednesday evening, the questions came rushing into my thoughts. Should I really show such a scripture to a prophet? What is he going to think of me? Will I be invited back to church?

So many questions rushed through my mind. I did not know what to do.

When I arrived at the house, I walked inside and greeted everyone. Afterwards, I spotted a chair in the back of the living room and sat down. I wanted to avoid close proximity in an effort that somehow, I would get the courage to not share the scripture with the pastor.

As he taught, I could not help but wonder if he was truly a false prophet. After all, he called himself a prophet and seemed to be honest and blameless, at least from my perspective.

I was raised to believe that anyone who held such an office must be truly a person of God. I did not want to view that any differently. It was almost sinful to do so, in my opinion.

The service had come to an end, and everyone was saying goodbye. I eased over to the pastor's son and confirmed again about sharing the scripture with his father. He reassured me to be obedient.

I glanced across the living room and noticed that the pastor was seeing off the last member. He closed the door behind her. That was my moment to present the scriptures to him in obedience.

"Excuse me, pastor," I said. "May I speak with you for a moment?" I asked. "Of course," he replied. "I've been thinking over what you prophesied to me last Sunday about me marrying your son," I said. "I want to obey the Lord, so I have been praying about the prophecy. A couple of nights ago, I had a dream. In the dream, this scripture was given to me by someone that I could not identify, except for the torso to the thighs," I said. "Oh?" he replied with surprise.

I handed him the Bible with it opened to the scripture. He read it for about 3 minutes, then slammed the Bible shut and handed it to me. He then walked away.

I was devastated. The most unusual, uneasy feeling overwhelmed me. I wondered if I had done something terrible to the man of God.

I looked over at the pastor's son, and he was staring at me with a concerned look. He then nodded his head as if to say, it was ok, I had done the right thing.

For a moment, I could not move from where I was standing. I knew that I had done something terrible. I could not remain in the house or on the property, so I left.

I left without saying goodbye to anyone, not even the son. I don't know how I walked from there to my father's friend's house, but I did.

I went straight to my room and dropped onto the bed. I wanted to pray but could not. I was in a state of shock.

I decided to get a place of my own, so I moved away from that neighborhood to another. I did not want to be in close proximity to the church, nor to anyone affiliated with it.

Discouragement and a feeling of abandonment were unbearable. The God that I trusted, and who revealed that scripture to me, had abandoned me, I believed.

That was the most unsettling feeling...a feeling of abandonment.

CHAPTER 26: GOD'S WORD PROVED TRUE AFTER ALL

Weeks turned into months, and months into years. I did not return to the neighborhood church. I was living on my own, and my time was spent working and examining my Christian journey.

Alabama was still fairly new to me, so friendship and social life were far and in between. I desperately wanted to be a part of a church body, but I had mixed feelings about how to go about doing so. I did not know which organization was the right one to join, nor did I have confidence in myself to know the difference.

Prayer was a part of my daily routine. That was all that I knew how to do well. I had developed a strong relationship with my manager at my place of employment, so that was really cool. She was quite friendly and compassionate, almost like a mother figure.

There was a young man who frequented the establishment quite regularly. One day, he gathered enough courage to ask me out on a date. My manager spotted him from afar, walked over to where the young man and I were having a conversation, and exclaimed, "Winsome, the blacker the berry, the sweeter the juice!"

I had no idea what she meant by that phrase until the day after. Apparently, she was trying to discourage me from getting into a relationship. She knew something that I didn't. She was a ball of fire. I was very thankful for her.

My initial encounter with her was out of desperation. After the situation that took place between the pastor and me, my trust in God was shattered. I stumbled upon my place of employment, where I remained for a few years. I did not know that it was a divinely inspired move until one day when a young man walked up to me and uttered these words:

"Winsome, is that you?" he asked.

My job title was head cashier. I was training someone on the register during a lunch rush. As the trainee and I worked the line, a young man approached the register and asked that question.

I did not recognize him initially until he asked the same question again, "Winsome, is that you?" His voice was familiar. It was the pastor's son.

I addressed him by his name in amazement. "How are you doing?" I asked. "It's been a while since we last saw each other!" I exclaimed. "Yes, it has," he responded. Almost relieved, it appeared. "You look so different. I am sorry, I did not recognize you," I continued. "I know," he replied. "I have a brain tumor, and I am on chemo, so I have gained a lot of weight," he continued.

Years ago, when I met him and his family, he was a slender young man. He had gained so much weight since then due to cancer treatment that I did not realize who he was.

"Oh my, I am so sorry to hear," I responded heartbrokenly. "It's alright, I trust in God," he responded.

It was lunch rush, so I had to cut the conversation short. He was a dear friend, and it hurt to see him in that condition.

A few weeks had passed, and I had another surprise. The pastor walked into my place of employment.

He and I made eye contact, and I froze. After all those years, I saw his son, and now, here was the father, the pastor. I did not know what was happening, but I was open to the Lord.

"Winsome, how are you?" he asked. "Hello. I am well, thank you," I responded. "You may be wondering why I am here talking with you, and I would understand why you feel that way," he continued. "My son (he stated his name) told me that he saw. I wanted to stop by and talk with you if you don't mind. I have something that I would like to tell you," he said. "Of course," I responded. "I will be getting off in half an hour. We could talk then," I said. "Sure, that would be great," he responded.

The next half hour seemed like an eternity. I could barely concentrate on my responsibilities. I did not know what was happening, but somehow, I had felt an indescribable peace inside of me, and I was a bit anxious as well. Oximoranism, I suppose.

So many questions dashed across my thoughts. Why was he here? What did he want to talk about? Lord, are you trying to tell me something? These questions and so many more raced through my mind.

I glanced over to where he was seated. He seemed to be restless. It was the end of my shift, so I clocked out and bade my manager goodbye. I walked over to where the pastor was seated.

He asked if he could take me home and talk on the way, but I decided that we should converse at the establishment, in a more secluded way. He agreed.

"Thank you for agreeing to talk with me, Winsome," he started off. "I've wanted to talk with you for quite some time now, but I did not have any contact information on you," he said. "You left abruptly years ago, and had no idea where you were," he continued.

I listened as he talked. I did not have much to say, and I did not want to interrupt him. I wanted to hear all that he had to say.

"Before my son died, he told me that he ran into you, here," he said. "I knew then that I must find you and tell you what I need to tell you," he continued. "Your son died!?" I exclaimed. "Yes, not too long ago," he said sadly. "He told me that he told you about his condition," he said. "Yes, he did. I am so sorry to hear," I said. "He was a good friend," I said. "Thank you," he said.

"Winsome, do you remember when you gave me those scriptures to read, years ago?" "Yes, I do," I replied. "They were true," he confirmed.

I broke down. I could not help tearing up. In that moment, my faith, trust, hope, and all that I had heard about God were solidified.

"Why did you slam shut the bible, then?" I asked. "I did not want to accept it," he said. "I am sorry for prophesying falsehood to you. I hope that you will forgive me," he said. "I have lost my marriage and my family," he continued.

I had compassion for him. "I cannot hold anything against you, sir," I said. "I am sorry for what you are experiencing," I continued. "It was good seeing you, and again, please forgive me," he said.

At that point, he walked away. It has been over 30 years now, and I have not seen him since.

I knew that God showed me that He, God, was and is faithful to His word. Praise His name.

CHAPTER 27: RENEWED FAITH AND A PROMISE TO SERVE

After I got home, prayer became my evening meal. I knelt down on the floor and began worshiping the Lord for showing me that it was He who had given me the dream years ago, and that the recipient was the right person because he confessed that he was a false prophet.

I also prayed for the pastor's family. A deep sadness overwhelmed me for what had happened to the son and the family at large. Additionally, I realize that God was faithful to His name. His name is holy, and it must not be taken in vain.

At that point, my faith increased so much that I vowed to serve Him no matter what. I was 23 years old and was ready to be married the right way.

Shortly after the encounter, I decided that it was time to start a family. I had visited a few churches in hopes of finding a church home. The customs in the churches were different from what I had known in Jamaica, so it was difficult to adapt.

After about a year or so, I met a young man who became my husband. He was also a part of the traditional Christian faith. We settled down and started a family.

Prior to getting married, I revisited the promise that I had made to God about getting married the correct or right way according to the typical customs or traditions of the Christian practice.

My to-be-husband and I had marriage counseling with a well-known pastor, a man of good reputation according to the church's customs prior to marriage. We practiced abstinence according to religious traditions. We did everything within our power to fulfill or carry out the traditions of pre-marital rituals in the sight of God and man.

So, why did the marriage fail? I asked myself.

Growing up in my hometown of Jamaica, I admired the lifestyles of the women in the churches. I had gotten baptized in a holiness church. My perception of the behavior of the women and their husbands was one that I aspired to have when I got married, I had hoped.

There was a certain respect and humility amongst the couples that sparked my attention. I admired it. I desired that type of marriage, so when I made the promise to God that I would be married the right way after the arranged marriage by my father, those were the things that I had in mind.

I had read the Bible a number of times, but I never truly understood how to interpret the scriptures. I was too much of an introvert who did not want to impede anyone, so I did not ask questions or get help from hardly anyone about the scriptures.

I read the first commandment: Thou shalt love the Lord thy God with all thy soul, all thy might and all thy strength (KJV), but I did not put emphasis on it. As a matter of fact, everything else took first place, including career and a good life.

Throughout the marriage, I practiced a Christian lifestyle as the rich young ruler who obeyed the commandments from his youth, but failed to practice the very thing that Jesus required, which was the first commandment.

On the contrary, I took bits and pieces of the scriptures and cleaved to what I thought were more befitting at the moment, according to current circumstances, so I did not seek God's guidance about my own life, nor did I have a relationship with Him; a very important part of the Christian journey.

What I clung to was the role of pastor, leader, or a guide. Someone who was chosen by God to model His ways or message to the church. That person, from my background, was a pastor, a male pastor.

The communities that I resided in, and the churches that I had attended, did not portray a female in the role of a pastor, so I did not readily embrace any other gender except a male's.

From that stance, I pivoted into viewing my own husband as the one whom God had in His stead to teach me about Him.

The reference scripture that I embraced that reflected my view was 1 Corinthians 13 vs 3: But I would have you know that the head of every man is Christ, and the head of the woman is the man, and the head of Christ is God. (KJV).

I could not fathom or think of entertaining the possibility of having a personal relationship or covenant with God for most of my Christian journey outside of a man.

There was a knowing or an understanding that the man of God or the pastor or the husband was the only one who heard from God, and then he funneled it to the congregation or the wife.

This belief was crafted at the core of my being, so much so that men became gods to me. It would have taken a broken relationship for me to repent to my God for having other gods before Him.

Throughout the 30-year marriage, my core focus was submission to my husband. I was raised by a father who took very good care of me. I had learned what it meant to honor a male, and I came to appreciate his hard work and dedication for my well-being.

When I got married, it was natural to lean on a man, a husband, to carry on what my father, in essence, had started.

In retrospect, I had not learned how to depend on God; I had learned how to depend on a man.

Yes, I worked both in and outside the home, and even got a master's degree, but I had not learned how to rely on God, nor did I have a personal relationship with Him. The truth is, I did not know that I had the freedom to do so.

As a professing Christian, I was in violation of the first commandment: Thou shalt love the Lord thy God with all thine heart, with all thy soul and with all thine heart (KJV).

Of course, I did not begin to entertain such truth until after a great loss. My quest for salvation was just that...for salvation...not to truly know God.

As far back as I could recall, I practiced all of the traditions and rituals that every church setting offered, including waiting to be married before starting a family.

Throughout the marriage, ministry, and church attendance were of utmost significance. Nothing was more important, even when the practices and rituals became forefront, not God nor His characteristics.

I lost myself in the marriage. The heart of a devoted person is true to what he deems to be of value...wherever that view or stance may derive from. This was my philosophy.

The core values that were embedded in me date back to my childhood/culture/religious upbringing. My mother was a homemaker, while my father worked outside the home. They both demonstrated a work ethic that was contagious not only to me, but to my siblings.

The residents around me all worked in some form or fashion to ensure that their loved ones were taken care of. Those who professed Christianity displayed an allegiance that was unmatched, at least in my opinion.

Those acts and duties formed me. Those core values were transferred to my marriage, family, and faith. Every facet of my being was dedicated to those three, regardless of what was going on around me.

There was a saying by those closest to me: "Whatever you set your mind to do, you were determined to accomplish it," I was often told. That was a true statement.

The misconception about that, though, was doing so without understanding or direction from the Holy Spirit.

In retrospect, my marriage of over thirty years was dissolved because of having the cart before the horse.

CHAPTER 28: FROM HEADSHIP TO HIS LORDSHIP

According to the National Institutes of Health (NIH), Christian marriages have a lower divorce rate when the faith is practiced from a selfless foundation. Historically, the common theme about Christian marriage dissolutions is due to one or both parties' faults, which, from a natural standpoint, is true.

The blame game becomes more dominant, which is a true sign that self-centeredness is foundational, not unselfishness, which is how true Christianity is intended to be.

I recalled the first time when I realized that something had gone terribly wrong in the marriage, but I did not do anything about it because of fear. Fear of violating my one-sided promise to God; fear of not keeping my commitment to what I had promised myself; fear of what others would say. I could go on and on.

I am a firm believer in the Holy Scriptures, in that they are the inspired Word of God. One in particular is headship. 1 Corinthians 11:3 — "the head of every man is Christ; and the head of the woman is the man; and the head of Christ is God." (KJV).

Personally, I desire to be covered. As stated before, that is my background, stemming from the covering of my father. Covering offers a form of protection and safety that I embrace.

I had not been in any other long-term relationships, nor was I on my own for long periods of time, so all I really knew was an interdependent relationship that spanned over 3 decades.

The implementation of headship in the relationship took precedence even over the first commandment and Godly love between a man and a woman, from my observations.

The scripture about man being the head of a woman, according to the Bible, needs insight and to be understood in order for it to be implemented as intended.

What took place in my marriage was not properly administered, which caused hurt and distrust between us. Most importantly, it caused great trepidation as it related to my faith and desire to do what was orderly according to God's order.

The zeal within me to follow the principles and order of God was so great that I inadvertently set aside God Himself. Instead, I focused more on being an obedient wife who was submitted to her husband, not on being led by the Holy Spirit.

In essence, something else had taken the place of God.

I recalled when that actually happened during the marriage. The spoken phrase "because I am the head" was used quite often to justify or nullify almost any decisions or ungodly behaviors.

At one point, I attempted to fix the situation, but ended up making things worse. By that time, my faith had been stoned, and I realized that I was alone, though I was married. Strange.

I should not have allowed things to have gotten that far, but I did. The decision to finally do something about it took over 3 decades.

A culmination of divine interventions, incidents, and even health concerns emerged, and I broke. The words that came to my desperate soul were "if I perish, I perish." With the echo of those words, I left the marriage.

The decision to leave the relationship was born out of courage and complete trust in the God that I had heard so much about, and who had revealed Himself in the most desperate situations in times past.

By His grace, He placed a few individuals in my path who sacrificed their time to help during such a vulnerable time of my life. I am very appreciative and grateful for their obedience to the Lord.

Prior to making such a decision, the Lord gave me a few reassuring scriptures. One of them was from the book of Exodus. The children of Israel were in bondage in Egypt for 430 years (KJV). During that time, they cried out to their God, who sent a deliverer, Moses, to deliver them.

I saw the mighty hand of God in a vision, delivering me from bondage as He did His people, the Jews.

Another scripture God gave me was from the book of John, chapter 5 (KJV). The man was paralyzed for 38 years until Jesus delivered him. That scripture was symbolic to my situation.

God hears the cry of His children, and He will not leave or forsake them. Thank you, Lord Jesus, for remaining faithful to your promises.

The foundation of being aligned or one with God the Father has been rooted in me since I was a child. The naivety of how to go about it caused me to stumble on the journey of faith.

In retrospect, the path that I took since being baptized at age 17 was one that was orchestrated by my father and God. I am seeing and appreciating this fact as I continue on this journey.

I have come to realize that there is no "blueprint," or perfect path to the end or the culmination of the walk of faith. It is truly a walk of faith.

Faith comes by hearing, and hearing by the word of God (Romans 10:17; KJV). This truth is available to all, and for the first time, I am approaching it with the guidance of the Holy Spirit.

Another important aspect of the walk of faith is the Holy Spirit. The Promise that Jesus made to His disciples before His ascension was that He would send the Holy Spirit back to earth to lead and guide them (us) into all truth. John chapters 14 and 16 (KJV).

Though this truth exists in the Holy Scriptures and is very obvious to all, it wasn't until the Holy Spirit revealed it to me that I became aware of it.

As a matter of fact, the listed scriptures were all revealed by the Holy Spirit to me. I must add that it was during desperate times during and after my marriage that I met the Lord. No other way.

Don't get me wrong, prayer and reading the Bible were how I survived during those desperate moments. However, the personal relationship that formed between the Lord and me was derived through the most troubling times of my life.

During those moments, the feeling of hopelessness, dread, and confusion overwhelmed me. I can relate to King David's prayer: "…yeah, though I walk through the valley of the shadow of death…" (Psalm 23, KJV).

Unlike the remainder of the scripture that he wrote, I feared evil; yet, the mercies of God brought me through by sending individuals to assist along the way.

Thank you, Lord Jesus, and may you continue blessing them to glory you.

CHAPTER 29: LEARNING TO SEE THROUGH HIS EYES

As I continue the walk of faith afresh in an unwed status, my reliance now is completely at the mercy and grace of our Lord and Savior Jesus Christ. I am now compelled to remain steadfast and determined, more so now than before.

The great thing is that this experience is of utmost importance. In other words, having a personal relationship with Christ is absolutely necessary for faith to accomplish its perfect work within me. The journey within me is the Holy Spirit that Jesus imparted to all who believe in Him.

I am learning to appreciate each experience that faces me. As a matter of fact, the 30-plus years of marriage were a learning experience. Rather than being bitter and throwing rocks, I constantly plead to the Holy Spirit to show me how to use those experiences to see Him more clearly.

How to see everything and everyone from His perspective, not mine, nor anyone else's. This is important. It is easy to conform and to live someone else's story. Doing so will not change who I am. I will only conform or mimic, which would be hypocritical.

Creating my own experiences, which in essence, is my own relationship with Jesus, comes only through me seeking Him with all of my heart. Doing so is not a bed of roses. Contrarily, it is a walk of death or giving up myself so that I can gain His identity.

His identity or characteristics are unselfish and benefit others. Period. My identity or characteristics are selfish and do not benefit others. It benefits me. This truth is difficult to face or admit, but it is what it is. There is no way around it.

Therefore, I agree with Paul when he stated: For me to live is Christ, and to die is gain (Phil. 1:21, Bible Hub).

This death (as I am experiencing) is excruciating. That is what being born again is. This revelation and adaptation should have been the beginning of my journey of faith. It was not, but God is merciful. He sees the sincerity and the desire within me to do so. He has mercifully allowed me to find Him, and I am determined to pursue Him.

As I navigate the next phase of this journey of faith, the realization of steadfastness and clarity from the Holy Spirit is most significant. This next phase is solo, in that I am not trying to attain a relationship, wealth, or even health from the Lord. Instead, the aim is to establish a relationship with Him.

Should He send any of the above or any other earthly goods, I pray that He will give me wisdom and understanding to not elevate them above Him.

It is His desire for His followers to inherit good things; however, it is not His desire for us to cling to them. I have learned a difficult lesson in placing "things" above Him.

He is truly a jealous God who wants complete loyalty to Him, and why not? He created man, woman, gold, diamonds, oil, copper, precious stones, and so forth that mankind desires. So, why not recognize the Creator of them all and exalt Him above His created things, correct?

In fairness, the previous question is easier said than done. I will elaborate. Some of the first teachings that I recall from a tender age of being identified as a child of God or a Christian was one's status of gain or wealth. Wealth was symbolic of God's blessings on a Christian.

As a matter of fact, that was the most sought-after objective to prove one's dedication as a Christian, other than escaping hell for heaven.

Growing up in a small town where reliance on farming for daily meals and sustenance was the norm, menial lifestyles were the norm. The small percentage of Christians who attained wealth were deemed more spiritual.

So you see, placing things or what one attained as earthly goods above the Creator was embedded in the core of one's belief as having "more" God.

Personally, I do not like attention. Wealth, in my opinion, attracts attention, so I strategically live below the radar and avoid a lifestyle that brings attention. This practice is more of a preference than a religious view.

As it relates to having a partner, the norm was to "find" one in the church, or find a Christian man or woman to marry. In other words, the attainment of stuff or things and gaining a wife or husband were heavily emphasised to depict God's blessings.

Attaining "things" was more significant than attaining a relationship with God.

In retrospect, the notion of having a relationship with the Almighty God was almost blasphemous from my point of view. The foundation or bases of any interaction with God were through a pastor. The pastor was the go-to person for everything pertaining to spiritual things.

It wasn't until I was in my early 30's when I finally embraced the idea of having a relationship with God the Father and His Son Jesus Christ.

I was involved in a non-denominational/non-traditional sect of about 25 individuals. The leader had decided that we would not have a meeting on a Sunday, as we had always had.

The consuming feeling of unfaithfulness to God for not fellowshipping gripped me terribly. I thought that God was mad at me for not gathering in a building with like-minded individuals. My whole faith-based or religious life was tied up in church attendance.

That was when it dawned on me that I needed to have a relationship with God for myself. Truth is, the thought was not readily embraced. I had to be convinced that it was okay to have a relationship with such an exalted being.

Establishing the proper personal-foundational relationship with such an awesome Being was borne out of desperation. I came to a lonely place in my spirit where the only place that I could go was to Him.

I had to find Him. I had to know Him. It was life or death for me because I had no B options.

I was not a smoker, alcoholic, nor was I addicted to anything, where I could ease the desire to belong. Those things were not a part of my coping mechanism, so I went to the only source that I knew. God.

I recalled getting on my knees in that 2-bedroom apartment and bawling. I did not know exactly why I was crying so passionately, but I knew how destitute I was.

I was a mother and wife with two toddlers. My duty was to the family and to God. Nothing else was significant outside of those two entities. That was a decision that I had consciously embraced.

CHAPTER 30: IT IS WITHIN ME

The directions of my then-husband were golden, so when he said to do, I did. That was how I followed the order of God, I told myself. My own thinking was in the hands of another, so having to establish a relationship outside of him was quite daring, but necessary.

As a matter of fact, it was a fight. My allegiance (as with my father) was shifting from a man, my husband, to His and my God. I began speaking up and expressing my views for the first time in the marriage. Of course, they were received as insubordination or in submissiveness.

The interesting thing was, I could not go back, spiritually, to where God had brought me from, though I was still married. Due to that fact, he and I received many counseling sessions from some of the men who were in the sect. Those sessions were numerous and lasted throughout several years of the union.

Still, my allegiance remained steadfast to the first commandment, which is to have no other gods besides the true God. Therefore, the battle continued. Metaphorically speaking, the great yacht that had been on a long journey was now being guided to another necessary path due to treacherous conditions. The journey must continue.

The relationship with God is one that is indescribable, except experienced. It trumps every other authority or role that mankind erects. It is so personal and needful that it puts life in perspective.

The intimacy of it creates a personal space that is proper, admirable, and right. As I spend this phase of the journey unwed, I have come to appreciate the one-on-one time that is allotted to my Creator.

As stated before, I did not readily embrace the initial loneliness that came with establishing such a relationship. It took some time for me to trust the process and believe that God would truly hear me.

In the past, God, to me, was somewhere in the sky, far above the clouds, and was unreachable except by special folks such as pastors. Those whose lives were completely surrendered to Him.

I knew that I was not in that category, so I had never conceived the notion that the likes of me could access such a God. The very thing that I was afraid of, abandonment of the very foundation that led me to be baptized, was where I was introduced to the Lord. A place of desperation.

I recall getting so low in my spirit that I grabbed my purse and was heading out the door to a friend's house one evening. It was as though God was not hearing me, and I felt like the room was closing in on me.

As I was heading down the steps, I heard a still voice that said, " It is within you.

I turned around and went back up the stairs. I sat down, and a calmness overwhelmed me. I began praying and crying out to the Lord, and thanking Him for showing up.

In that moment, many things were born, including the title of this book. God's spirit had come up in me and reminded me that He was enough for me. My faith spiked in that moment, and I was eternally grateful for His mercy.

I must admit that faith is scary to me. Maybe it's because I don't fully understand it. A special friend has told me numerous times that faith without works is dead, indeed. I am starting to believe it.

Until the Holy Spirit prompted me on that momentous day, I did not understand that He speaks directly to me, not only through others. It is quite reassuring to understand this truth.

Life has become more meaningful since that experience. Talking to the Father is similar to talking to someone who cares for me. It's intimate and special. I am not afraid to tell Him about my deepest fears and highest moments.

In those quiet moments, if I listen intently, I can hear the Lord speaking. It could be as simple as preparing a meal, and He may tell me to check the door because I may have left the keys in it.

I recall a situation that happened recently. I went to a busy shopping center where I used the restroom. When I got to my destination, I realized that I did not have my phone. I began to panic. Immediately, I jumped in the car and headed back to the location.

On the way there, I prayed. A calmness encompassed me that I could not explain. I began playing different scenarios in my mind as to what could be going on with the phone; yet I could not help remaining calm.

When I walked inside the store, I was prompted to ask an associate if someone had turned in a cell phone. He advised me to check with customer service.

The initial thought was to check the restroom first since that was where I left it, but instead, I listened to the voice of the Holy Spirit.

As I entered the customer service area, my eyes landed on a phone on the back counter that looked similar to mine. I walked up to the front counter and asked if someone had turned in a lost phone.

The worker said yes, and that I should prove to her that it was mine. She handed the phone to me, and immediately it recognized my face ID.

I dropped to my knees right then and there and thanked God for His guidance.

Had I lost that phone, especially at that hour, and with everything else that I had going on, plus work the following day, it would have posed a huge inconvenience in so many ways.

That was one recent example of listening to the Holy Spirit.

I must admit that a relationship with God through Jesus Christ truly is a faith walk. The last few months have proven it over and over. Sometimes all that I could say was let your will be done.

There was and is no second option for me. Yes, it is taking everything out of me to not worry, not fret, just trust and believe that He is a man of His word.

I recall a scripture taken from the King James Version of the Bible: Psalm 138:2: God has magnified or (elevated) His Word above all His name.

My interpretation of this scripture is that God keeps His Word at all costs unless He decides to do something differently. My only responsibility to such a God is to listen intently for Him and believe Him or do what He says.

One of the most amazing traits that I have experienced about God is His attraction to obedience. This trait takes me back to when I was under my father's care.

Daddy was not a person of great wealth; yet, the sacrifices that he made for my well-being were on account of my obedience to him. He was a man of few expectations, but they were very important to him.

So it is with God, I have noticed. He does not ask much of us, but what he asks is usually very significant.

My father had good intentions for me. I did not know exactly what those intentions were. As I obeyed him, his visions or plans became apparent.

Those interactions with my father were/are similar to the relationship that I have with the Lord. He always has good intentions for those who are obedient to Him.

As I travel on this path of faith, it is becoming more apparent that no one, not even a parent, spouse, or child, can walk it for me.

As the scripture declares, "And whoever does not carry his cross and follow me cannot be My disciple" (Luke 14:27, Bible Hub).

This is a true statement.

CHAPTER 31: WALKING AWAY TO TRULY WALK WITH GOD

One of the most amazing truths that has been inadvertently made known to me was the fact that, though I spent all those years in organized religion, it was not until I reluctantly walked away from it that I began establishing a relationship with God. Amazing, right? Yes, it's true. Through life's experiences and disappointments, I have come to realize that God is not a pretender and that He doesn't like bribes. I realize that much of what I was in and under was based on traditions and manmade rituals. They kept me in great bondage and pretence. I could never be my authentic self, which is what God wants, so that He can transform such a nature into His. I am seeing more and more that He truly delights in transformation.

I have also discovered that what my religious background says is sin is really not how God sees it. Isaiah 55:8-9 declares: For my thoughts are not your thoughts, neither are your ways my ways, saith the Lord. For as the heavens are higher than the earth, so are my ways higher than your ways, and my thoughts than your thoughts (KJV).

As a child, I recall feeling so condemned when I told a lie or made a mistake. On one occasion, I was washing dishes, and the drinking class broke and cut my right thumb. Rather than taking care of the bleeding, I began worrying about the glass. How disappointing it was to have broken the glass. The task of doing almost everything right was quite burdensome. Doing everything right was aligned with my religious views and the expectations of perfection. The scripture above was always in my thoughts, but I did not know how to appropriate it, so I kept on doing what I knew how to do, and that was to keep doing what I had always done…followed my traditions and rituals.

As I reflected on my failed marriage, I had so many questions. Didn't I follow the expectations of seeking a man who was a Christian before I got married? Yes, I did. Didn't I get sound counseling from an experienced pastor before I got married? Yes, I did. Didn't I wait to be married before having children? Yes, I did. The above questions derived from the religious foundation that I esteemed to the very core of my being. So why did the marriage fail? These questions were prominent in my thoughts years before the actual annulment. The truth was (and is) that those questions were legitimate, and the principles were honorable. However, God does not tamper with the will.

Out of desperation, the Holy Spirit revealed a most powerful truth to me. The will is a gift or freedom or a part of God's being that is so powerful, yet subtle that it is easily overlooked. As I dove into gaining understanding from the Source (God), I have discovered (and continue to discover) that that is one thing that God does not tamper with. It is a part of Him that makes Him who He is. Scripture declares that He made us in His own image, in the book of Genesis. A major part of the image of God within us is the freedom of the will.

During the marriage, I inadvertently exercised my will to endure certain conditions that were contrary to my core beliefs; however, I labeled my will as endurance, keeping my vows despite what was taking place, or attempting to carry out the expectations of others. I did not realize that those acts were a part of my will, not God's, as I convinced myself. Contrarily, God's ways or commandments were the complete opposite. In other words, the fruits/behavior were vastly different from the written words, or from how the Word tells us to treat one another.

Now that I have been convinced by the Holy Spirit that will is a very significant factor in the walk of faith, I have taken on a completely different view of the journey of faith.

This new view, the will, allows me to take accountability for my own walk and actions. It is liberating; yet, costly. Costly in the sense that the decisions that I make from now on will be of my own doing, not someone else's. That's where liberation is borne. That's where accountability is formed.

On this quest of establishing a relationship with my Creator, He is revealing who He is to me. It's almost unbelievable how much freedom is in Him. His ways contradict the very religious, traditional, ritualistic performances that I was completely devoted to. Those rituals kept me in bondage and fear that were crippling. Despite the scriptures that talked about freedom in Christ, I overlooked them all in order to keep my traditions.

As I reflect on why I ignored the very freedom that Jesus offers, the only conclusion that I came to was fear. Fear of doing what He said because I would have gone against my traditions. From my view, the traditions were more significant than what the Word says. That's the truth.

I have since come to realize that religion is just what it is… religion…not faith. I have defined religion as a set of ritualistic rules that are independent of faith. The Inspired Word (s) of God declares that without faith, it is impossible to please God. (Hebrews 11:16[NIV]). Based on this scripture, ritualistic rules will not allow me to please God. Why would I continue to adhere to such rituals?

I appreciated the self-restraint that my religious foundation offered me at a young age. Where I errored was when I grew up, or was more knowledgeable about transitioning from that foundation to one of spirit or faith, I did not embrace it. Instead, I remained until I was engulfed in my traditions so much so that I could not hear the Holy Spirit, which was (and is) the core of freedom.

As a matter of fact, I recall the time when I did not go to church for a few weeks. I was in a relationship, and my partner at the time decided that the family would take a break from fellowshipping for a while. Great anxiety, coupled with tremendous guilt and fear, overwhelmed me to the point of thinking that I had committed an unpardonable sin. I had broken allegiance to my religion, and it was not a good thing, I thought.

As I reflected on the very foundation of what I held dear for over 4 decades, I questioned why I chose to remain in such bondage rather than embracing freedom. During pre-adulthood, there was no accountability for my actions, where going to hell or heaven was concerned. It was easy to assume that my age or immaturity was a huge factor, and probably so. Afterall, God was navigating the ship of salvation, so all I had to do was chill while being mindful not commit those five major sins.

The salvation that I had received from a young age was one that was entangled with guilt, fear, and self-abasement. In other words, bondage. There was no room for the Holy Spirit. As a matter of fact, the Holy Spirit was deemed as a gift of speaking in tongues, not as a Helper, as the Bible states. Speaking in tongues was a sign of leveling up, or arriving somewhere spiritual.

After over 40-years of exhaustion and trying to attain salvation or

a place with God, circumstances caused me to discover my own will, which gave room to accountability.

CHAPTER 32: FREEDOM THROUGH THE WILL

The revelation of the will by the Helper, the Holy Spirit, coupled with the written word of God, was the most significant revelation of my Christian journey. One of the reasons these revelations are significant is the accountability aspect of them. Being able to make decisions about my life and the direction that I want it to go in was and is very liberating. For instance, I can decide to visit a worship center of any denomination without worrying about offending anyone. I can also decide not to visit without any condemnation. This new approach allows me to make decisions that are inspired by my own free will/spirit as opposed to obligations, rituals, and customs. It also allows for Jesus Christ to be my Lord as opposed to a man or a pastor. I have become aware that the discovery of the will grants freedom with accountability. These are inseparable.

Yes, it is for freedom that Christ sets us free, but freedom must not be used to satisfy the flesh (Gal. 5:13 NIV). This is a hard saying because what I deem as spiritual may not be what Jesus deems as spiritual. The scripture clearly declares for my thoughts are not your thoughts, neither are your ways my ways, saith the LORD. For as the heavens are higher than the earth, so are my ways higher than your ways, and my thoughts than your thoughts (Isaiah 55:8-9, KJV). My interpretation of this scripture is that, though I am free in Christ Jesus to exercise my own God-given will, because I yield myself to Him first, whatever He says trumps what I say or do.

This does not mean that I am not free to live my own life; it simply means that if I choose (my will) to live for Christ, or adopt His characteristics, I am in essence demonstrating my agreement to allow my will to be fluid enough to say "yes Lord, not my will, but yours be done. This is another difficult stance; yet, necessary if I want to live as Christ lived.

Before the revelation of the will, one of the greatest deceptions that I experienced was living my life, believing that I was yielding myself to Jesus Christ as my Lord. I was not. Instead, I yielded myself to my traditions and to the expectations of others, not for Christ. I spent countless hours praying and pleading to God to show me why I was so confused and frustrated with my walk of faith. It was not supposed to be strenuous, fearful, and obligatory, but it was.

The crazy thing was, I truly believed that I was sharing the sufferings of Christ, so I kept enduring unfavorable conditions. I did so because, in essence, that was how I justified my actions. At one point, I was detached from my family for over a decade. It was one way to prove to God that I had forsaken mother, father, sister, and brother for His sake. The funny thing was, I had to eventually return to them for consolation when the very headship of that faith I had forsaken them for put me out of our home.

I had to make sense of it somehow. I had gone too far to turn back, I would often say to myself. Friends and family members advised me to make sense of my life. At one point, someone said to me, "What would your father say about your current condition if he were alive?" I had no response. I was in denial, I suppose, or I was completely deceived.

I had proposed in my heart that I was going to keep my promise to God, so I was determined to continue what I had committed to. By then, there were so many factors to consider, such as young children, career, and most importantly, the Christian marriage. Those things were extremely important, so dedication and commitment were unquestionable. I purposed in my heart before God to be a model mother and wife, not only as a Christian woman, but also as an example for my children. That was very important to me, especially for the girls. I wanted them to have a reference for their own lives.

In the back of my mind, I was breaking. They had witnessed turmoil of arguments and disarray in the Christian marriage, and it churned the very core of my being. My way of making things "calm" was to take a drive or disappear in another part of the house. I did not want them to continue experiencing a Christian woman behaving in such a manner.

Inward wrestling of the very essence of my being became a way of life. It became normal. It's amazing what the body can be subjected to once it's aligned with the spirit! My mindset had become accustomed to abnormality to the point where I had lost my own sense of direction. I was lost.

I recall speaking to a dear friend about my situation. I stated to her that I could see myself in the spirit, walking to my doom. By that time, I had lost weight to the point where I thought that I had an illness. I had gone to my family doctor for a check-up, and all went well. I knew then that the condition was spiritual. In the spirit, I saw myself giving up, and I did not know how to recover from that state.

Throughout it all, I never stopped trusting God. I had no B options. If he had not come through, I would have perished.

God, by His grace and mercy, miraculously delivered me from myself and the situation with a handful of individuals who had His Word in them. He blew my mind.

God blew my mind in that the way He delivered was not how I was expecting Him to. He sent His Word by one of the few individuals who said to me: You shall know them by their fruits (Matthew 7:15, NKJV). Immediately, my spiritual eyes were opened. Scenarios after scenarios flashed through my mind. Those scenarios depicted instances of fruits within the marriage that were in complete contrast to Christ's characteristics and what he taught during His ministry on earth.

I began to weep profusely. In one of those scenarios, the Lord showed me that His order of headship, God is the Head of Christ, Christ is the head of man, and man is the head of woman, was taken out of context by someone who was placed in the role of a husband. The Holy Spirit's revelation was specific to an abuse of authority, and that He had no pleasure in such. The fruits were not Christ-like.

In that very moment, the wisdom of God, coupled with strength and determination, propelled me to do something about my plight. It did not take an army for deliverance, only a few faithful souls and obedience to the Spirit. Praise His name.

My spirit began to experience liberation. Liberation that is now allowing me to seek first His kingdom, which, in essence, I am seeking the Creator to know Him on a personal level. One that is intentional and authentic. This is actually the first commandment.

For the first time, I am beginning to get to know my God, and it is amazing. The liberation that I am experiencing has everything to do with my desire, coupled with my will to know the truth, which is where freedom lies.

CHAPTER 33: LIBERATION A JOURNEY OF TRUST IN CHRIST

This newfound liberation is inspiringly exciting. An excitement that challenges the very core of fear. Because I am determined to trust in God, not man, nor myself, I am watching my faith increase daily. This journey is an adventure that is filled with the unknown. The truth is, this current state was what I dreaded throughout my adult life. I had read about faith in the book of Hebrews, and I could not imagine a complete trust in a being that I could not see.

For most of my life, there was someone whom I could literally depend on for support. It began with my father, transitioned to pastors, then to a husband. There was hardly a time when I was independent and had to rely completely on God, with understanding. This time is now. I am, however, a firm believer that God works through His creation, people in particular. As a matter of fact, I have experienced such throughout my life, and I honor God through them. Amen.

As it stands now, with my whole heart and by God's unmerited grace, I have set my heart to discover God through His only begotten Son, Jesus Christ. I am looking forward to giving up all pretences and falsehood just to know the true God. I have walked away from worldly security that would have kept me in bondage and fear. Bondage and fear are not from the Father.

The past year has been quite adventurous. I have watched my faith blossom from a mustard seed to an acorn (smile). Each step has been strategically applied with intention. My eyes are focused on the voice of the Holy Spirit, the Helper whom Jesus promised to send back after He was ascended to heaven. Each prayer, each step must be led by the Holy Spirit, not anyone else's. Not even mine.

I am currently being molded by His discipline to train my spirit to be as His. This is my goal, and it is intentional. I am aiming to be transformed into His image, and it's a transformation, indeed. At times, it is excruciating because the flesh or familiarity is quick to resist. Like Paul, the Apostle, I am leaving those things behind, and I am pressing on to the mark/goal of the high calling, which is completely selling out to Christ Jesus.

My aim is to agree with the Apostle Paul, who, with confidence, states that he is crucified with Christ, yet not he, but Christ who lives in him. The life that he now lives in the flesh, he lives by faith in the Son of God who loved him and gave himself for him. This is my aim.

This journey of liberation or freedom in Jesus is one that is lonely and has caused me to be an outcast. It is forcing me to be genuine, real, and authentic, which totally eradicates religious rituals, manmade traditions, and rules, the epitome of falsehood and pretence. Freedom in Christ for me means that those who have come to know me to be one way may now see me differently.

A prime example of this transformation is standing up for what is just. I will not allow anyone to cause me to compromise my beliefs because they may not conform to manmade traditions or expectations that fit a certain norm. I may decide, for instance, to disagree with a person's lifestyle for one reason or another. However, because that person is made in God's image, which means that person is accountable to His or her creator, not to me.

My responsibility in such an encounter would be to demonstrate mercy rather than condemnation in order to win over such a one. Under the traditional rudiments that I freed myself from, my approach to such a person would have been great self-righteous judgment and condemnation that would not testify to Christ's nature or characteristics. That approach would have been a complete contradiction of the true gospel that states that God desires mercy, not sacrifice.

Because mankind is created in the image of God, a Christ-like response to anyone who demonstrates anti-Christ's characteristics should be viewed with much mercy, considering ourselves first. Unless we all can declare that we are guiltless. If no one needs salvation, then why did God send His only begotten Son to be the ultimate sacrifice? The very thought of Jesus' sacrifice should be enough for mercy to be extended, rather than condemnation.

This liberation that I am encountering has made room for complete trust or faith in Jesus Christ, which has always been my aim. Interestingly, had I not gone through what I did only a year ago, I would not have been in this space. This space is personal. It allows the relationship between the Holy Spirit and me to be cultivated, thus bearing fruit.

Bearing fruit, good fruit, is very significant to the Christian walk or the way. This is how I will know that I am of Christ. The most interesting thing about this liberation, or a journey led by the Holy Spirit, is the discovery of me. The real me.

As stated previously, I've had a sheltered life. My dependency was reliant on someone else, a father, husband, or pastor. I am grateful for a life that was less difficult in terms of provisions. Provisions are of the Lord, so I do not take them for granted. Headship is also from the Lord, and I enjoy the security, safety, and provisions that a husband who walks in the proper order provides.

What I failed to realize was my responsibility to ensure that I had an individual relationship with the Father. I thank God for His abundant grace for this current opportunity to establish a relationship with Him. This is most significant as it pertains to salvation. No one can give an account of my actions or behavior except me; therefore, establishing a relationship with the Father is the only way for accountability to be established. Thus, the word liberation.

Liberation, for me, is finding myself. For the first time in over 4 decades, I am confronting or facing Winsome. I am discovering that I do have a will. A will that I can exercise however I please. I am also aware that there are consequences to exercising my God-given will despite the outcome.

In the Book of Genesis, God states that He made man in His own image. One significant part of that was the will that He imparted to mankind. He made us free beings...like Himself. Of course, that will become restricted after the fall in the book of Genesis. Thus the Law.

The Law (depicted in the Old Testament) restricted mankind from his will in order to protect him. Mankind was using his freedom abusively. That was not the intent; therefore, God had to implement a governance (the Law) to protect mankind from himself.

Nevertheless, it can be restored through Jesus if mankind yields himself to exercising his will for the intent that it was originally given. This is the epitome of restoration or freedom in Christ Jesus. Since God, through Christ, has granted me grace to exercise this freedom, I intend to use it for what it was intended to do.

With steadfastness and determination, I have now set my heart to search out the Kingdom of heaven or the heart of Jesus Christ just to get to know who I am in Him, and how to relate to Him and creation. I am excited, yet cautious because I do not want to get entangled in any yoke of bondage that distracts this quest.

CHAPTER 34: LEARNING TO LOVE GOD ABOVE ALL

One of the first things that I am seeing about myself on this journey is being intentional about prioritizing. I live in a society where buying and selling are a way of life. Natural provisions such as shelter, meals, and means to make a living are essential. I am also aware of the spiritual part of this equation that is very significant. How do I put these two natures or aspects in perspective, I asked myself. Since I agree with the teachings of Jesus, I embrace His message about seeking first the kingdom of heaven. Well, how do I approach that? I asked myself.

As I search the scriptures, I notice that there are numerous strategies that are detailed about both the natural and the spiritual worlds. How do I make sense of how to implement those directives within my life? The Holy Spirit (The Helper, John 14:26 NASB) is the main source that interprets the scriptures. I am learning how to rely on Him to guide me. The truth is, this is not something that I am familiar with, so it's causing me to exercise patience. Patience is a fruit of the spirit, as the book of Galatians states, so I am embracing the waiting.

God knows, and I know that I have responsibilities to tend to. Children, job, paying bills, sharing my resources with others, and so forth. I also have my spiritual life to mold. As I embrace the first and second commandments: Thou shalt love the Lord your God with all your heart, soul and mind and your neighbor as yourself (Matthew 22: 37-40, KJV). By the way, before I can even begin to love my neighbor as myself, it is of utmost importance to learn how to love God first.

The Holy Spirit's interpretation of that scripture is to simply remain in the teachings of Christ and to learn about His characteristics as are evident in the New Testament. Loving the Lord

God with all my heart, soul, and mind simply means acknowledging Him above all else. Doing so is not a performance or foolish gesture. It's not simply quoting something that someone experienced or even reciting a few bible verses. It's not practicing rituals, working my fingers to the bones to abase myself, or even being a "good" girl.

To love God simply means to surrender, yield, submit, or present myself to Him wholly and completely. He does not force, threaten, or condemn me if I do not. Man-made ritualistic practices are contrary to being led by the Holy Spirit. I recalled living under great condemnation if I intentionally or unintentionally broke one of the rules or rituals in such organizations. There was no room for grace because it's not possible for one to demonstrate grace if they do not know what it is.

According to Merriam-Webster's dictionary, grace is defined as a God-given virtue (self-denial, humility, and love). The only deity that can convey grace is God. Therefore, if one is seeking his own agenda, how can he offer grace that comes only from an outside source? It's impossible. It is clear to see that unless Godly principles establish an organization that professes Him, it's not possible for such to demonstrate any fruits of the spirit, which include grace.

Because I am yielding myself to God, He is allowing me to see Him for who He is and how He wants me to see Him. As a Father, not as a master.

Merriam Webster's dictionary defines the father as: one who attends to with care, governor, overseer, protector. Because God demonstrates such characteristics towards me first, by my actions or lifestyle, I demonstrate to Him that I am grateful for His love towards me.

As I allow myself to discover or know the true essence of God the Father, the Holy Spirit, or the Helper is beginning to introduce Him to me in a most simple yet intimate way. He directed me to the book of Genesis, where I re-read a few significant verses. Some of those relevant verses detailed how God made heaven and earth. Mind you, I read those verses several times; however, when I re-read them this time, my understanding began to form.

The Holy Spirit confirmed that God made heaven and earth while He revealed why He made them as such. With tears of joy for God's unmerited favor towards me, I write the following. The Holy Spirit showed me that the reason why He made this beautiful planet the way that He did is because of the love that He has as a Father and a Provider for us.

His love is demonstrated in the very things that are created and that are consumed by animals and mankind for survival and for our pleasure. The very elements that provide the air that we breathe were strategically designed so that His plants, animals, and mankind can stay alive. The system as a whole coexists as a unit strategically for mankind to benefit from because of the Father's love for us.

To bring home the point, mankind or humans is recorded as the only creation made in the very image of God. What does this fact say about God's love and admiration for us? This truth alone should solidify any doubts of unconditional love for mankind by an amazing Father without any effort on our part. In other words, God's provision for mankind is independent of us. We did not have to do anything to be bestowed such honor.

Seeing that I cannot deny these truths of such generosity without any effort on my part, wouldn't it be a fair question to ask myself, why wouldn't I reciprocate by being kind to each other and the planet as an appreciation to the Giver? In essence, this approach is basically what God is asking us to do in the first two commandments. Out of appreciation for what He has done for us, based on what our eyes can literally behold, all He asks of us is to appreciate His kindness by acknowledging Him and treating His creation with gratitude.

This is as simple as I can state it. It's really an amazing thing to discover the heart of my Father. I used the personal pronoun my because this quest is indeed personal. Another revelation of this beautiful Being is how simple He is. As I search Him out in scriptures, I am seeing more and more clearly that all He desires of me is true recognition that He truly exists and that He is the mastermind behind what is clearly obvious for all to see. I cannot disagree.

I liken God's passion for true acknowledgement by His most valued creation, mankind, to an artist. If an artist painted a picture that represented something quite meaningful, wouldn't he want to be acknowledged for his work? Absolutely! Why would God be any different? Would God not have made that artist who wanted to be acknowledged? Isn't God due much more honor than a man? If yes, why would I give more honor to the created thing than to the Creator?

God does not need validation from anyone. He stands supreme. He has no rivals. None from the beginning of time, nor will there be any other who can lay claim to what is obvious. Yet, He desires true worship, honor, and gratitude from His handiwork. That is not too much to desire.

CHAPTER 35: DISCOVERING GOD WITHIN ME

For the life of me, I do not understand how I have made the very essence of my existence so complicated. As I ponder over that realization, in all honesty, I was trying to attain something. I was trying to attain a status or a place with God. In other words, I bought into the fallacy that salvation could be attained through works.

The Bible states that faith without works is dead (James 2:17). Here, I see that faith must be accompanied by works for faith to be active. The work alone is simply that...works. That approach is invalid as it pertains to salvation. In other words, I cannot be received by God the Father based on my performance. Only faith in God. Performance is man-initiated, while faith with works is Christ's initiated.

I spent most of my life doing the best I could to the first. It caused much disappointment and discouragement. At one point, I thought that God Himself abandoned me. I could not do enough to be "right with him," and it devastated me. I recalled being so overly anxious that I had shunned myself from even reading the Bible. I did not want to hear anything about the same old do this, do that.

For instance, for over 3 decades, I put everything that I had into submitting to my ex as the head of household according to the chain of command that is evident in the Bible. I had mastered everything else that a wife and mother could by works or performance. That still was not sufficient. I was exhausted.

I spent numerous hours crying out to God to help me to just get that one last thing mastered, complete submission to my ex. I desperately wanted to please God through His natural order of submission. Anything that I did was still not enough. I did not know what else to do. At that point, I thought that God Himself was disappointed in me. I could not bear the thought of disappointing

Him; yet, I was doing nothing to change my circumstances. The truth is, I did not know how to.

I did not envision the union ending so that I could find salvation. It was not something that was preplanned, though I saw the handwriting on the wall. Yes, there were many instances where I noticed that the foundation of my belief within the union was not built on Christ (love), but somehow, I'd hoped that it would miraculously get there. It did not.

Out of desperation, God, by His grace and mercy, revealed to me that the only foundation that stands is one that is built on love, not works. Mine was work or performance, and it had to be torn down.

This journey of self-discovery is causing me to go back to the true essence of my own existence. One that forces me to truly examine the reason for being created and the purpose of my life. This journey is forcing me to put things in perspective, away from any outside force.

All my life, I obeyed rules and regulations that shaped my natural life. Doing so created self-discipline, an essential trait that lends to living a lawful civil life. When I began pursuing religion, I began to discover that these two worlds were different. One is governed by force or man-made ordinances, while the other is governed by divine order or ordinances.

It took me to this point in my life to realize that these two worlds or kingdoms are governed by different kings. The man-made one is ruled by a lower king, while the other is ruled by the King of kings. Once the Lord allowed me to realize the difference between the two, with fierce determination, I decided to abandon everything of the lower kingdom in order to pursue Jesus.

By doing so, another revelation that He granted me was that He,

Jesus, dwells within me. What a revelation! I recall that moment when I got the revelation. It was in the summer of 2025. I had gotten off work and was settling in for the evening. After preparing dinner, I showered and began watching the evening news.

All of a sudden, an intense, lonely space enveloped me. I wanted to pray, but the space seemed to impede my concentration. I had a dear friend who lived about 10 minutes away, so I decided to visit with her for a bit. She was a person whom I could talk with about Godly things because she possessed a gift of discernment that I recognized.

As I grabbed my purse and began walking down the stairs, a small reassuring voice spoke to my spirit and said, The same God that is in Miss Annie is in you. Miss Annie is my dear friend. Immediately, I stopped, turned around, and went back upstairs.

When I got to the top of the stairs, I dropped my purse, fell on my knees, and began praying and crying to my Lord. I knew that He spoke those words to my spirit because they resonated. It was at that moment that the title of this book was born.

For the first time, I had come to realize that the same God whom my friend, Annie, served for all those years, He was also within me. By the way, it was around the same time that the Holy Spirit allowed me to tap into the will. That was when my true identity was discovered.

My true identity, the essence of who I really am, is found in my Creator in whose image I was created. That significant discovery is propelling me to keep going. Keep seeking. Keep discovering who I am. This discovery is truly liberating.

The New Testament speaks of this freedom that can only be found in Jesus. I read those scriptures many times, but I was unable to tap into that freedom. The Holy Spirit granted access to me because I was seeking God's heart.

There was a time when I sought God to get something from Him. That's the absolute wrong foundation, but that was what I knew. That was the foundation on which I got baptized. One of the reasons why I got baptized at such a young age was that I did not want to go to hell. This reason may seem understandable, because after all, who wants to go to hell?

When the Lord revealed my foundation, I then realized that my motive for joining the church was not based on knowing God. Instead, it was based on getting something from Him. As I examined myself further, I discovered a number of things that I wanted from God. At that point, I felt ashamed.

I was ashamed of taking advantage of God's goodness. It is His good pleasure to bless those whose hearts are truly seeking Him, both naturally and spiritually; however, those tangible blessings do not offer satisfaction because loving God first is the only basis for satisfaction.

This is how I come to know Him in me, and me in Him. That's the epitome of a marriage that Paul himself described in his teachings. With such a conviction, I have since set my heart to seek Him at all costs. In doing so, He is revealing himself to me in ways that I could not have fathomed until now.

I am convinced that these revelations would not have been revealed until I made that decision to seek God's kingdom, rather than what God could only do for me. Seeking Him first about everything, small or great, is truly a stretch of faith. I have to discipline myself to adjust to this new experience.

Everything that I undertake from the summer of 2025, when God visited me in a tremendous way, has been completely by faith in God through Jesus Christ alone. Every person or circumstance that I encounter is on account of trusting God with all of my heart, soul, and mind. My whole being is going through a transformation.

In some circumstances, I can literally feel the burning or suffering as the flesh is being crucified. It's excruciating at times. One thing that I am noticing is the peace that comes with relying on Him despite what I am experiencing. It's truly amazing.

In the culture that I was brought up in, carrying a grudge against someone who offended me was normal. That practice was a dominant part of my upbringing. On this new quest, the Holy Spirit revealed the embedded practice that had taken residence in my heart since I was a child.

The interesting thing about the revelation was that I was shocked when the Lord revealed it. I thought that because I was a professing Christian, that would automatically disappear. Not so. In my recent past, someone committed some things against me. I was bitter against that person. Though I read in the scriptures that I should not practice such acts, it felt better to hold a grudge against the person.

When the Lord revealed my heart to me, I despised what I saw. I did not want that type of fruit to represent me anymore, so I asked the Lord for His wisdom to rid myself of it.

CHAPTER 36: TRANSFORMATION THROUGH TRIALS

The interesting thing was that the embedded trait that haunted me since childhood did not just magically disappear because I asked the Lord for wisdom to rid myself of it. No. Contrary to what my ritualistic man-made religious traditions taught me, I was actually placed in situations where I was faced with the choice or option to continue being resentful or rid myself of resentment. During those trying situations, it felt as though there was a tearing or a war taking place inside of me. A war for my soul. Interestingly, I could also sense peace as I recalled scriptures such as I can do all things through Christ who strengthens me. In those moments, the Holy Spirit was in the battle with me, so I was not alone. He honored His inspired scriptures as I stood on them. After a few scenarios, resentment and bitterness were transformed into forgiveness and forbearance. That's the power of the Holy Spirit when one determines in his heart to be transformed into the image of God.

On this journey of discovering who I am in Christ and my responsibility as one who is made in His image, by His faithfulness to His word that says if I seek Him, I will find Him, I have discovered a great deception that has been planted in me from a teaching that I heard while listening to a sermon. The great deception was (is) that once I decided to give my life to Christ and join the church, God would do everything for me from that point on.

In other words, as long as I went to church and stayed away from the these sinful acts: sexual immorality, drinking, smoking, lying, stealing, listening to worldly music and I did not wear any other jewelry except a wedding band and I did not get my hair relaxed, I was okay with God; therefore, I was destined for heaven. For as long as I could remember, I tried my best not to violate those ordinances. As I continued attending church, more man-made ritualistic laws were enacted. By then, I became exhausted trying to keep them.

When I migrated to the U.S., I went straight back under another form of "touch not taste not." I still could not perform well enough, so I ended up abandoning everything that I was taught from childhood, which led me to where I am today. At that point, I had stopped reading the Bible. The approach that I took would have been considered an abomination and a disorder to my organized religious upbringing.

I began looking at the creation itself and said within my heart, whoever created such an awesome earth must be worth searching out. Trips to remote areas of the city where I reside, such as recreational areas and bodies of water, connected me. I began experiencing oneness with their originality. There, I would pray and invite the Designer of it all to speak to me. I needed to hear from Him. I needed to find Him. I would have gone insane had He not answered my cries.

He began making Himself known to me in dreams, people, animals, trees, flowers, and so forth. Most significantly, He opened my eyes to see the scriptures as they were intended to be seen. He revealed that the scriptures were never designed for profit or gain, but for edification. They were not designed for condemnation, but for freedom. Not for brutality, but for mercy and grace. They were inspired by the Holy Spirit to introduce mankind to Him.

As I peeled through the scriptures, it is clear that God's motive from the beginning is to have a relationship with people. The sacrifice of His Son, Jesus, was the ultimate blood sacrifice, based on nothing else but love for mankind. I had read scripture: For God so loved the world that He gave His only begotten Son, that whosoever believeth in Him, should not perish, but have eternal life (John 3:116, KJV), many times, but did not understand what it truly meant until my recent quest.

After reading said scripture, I searched out others that talked about love. I desperately wanted to truly understand the heart of God, so I went on a deep search. During my search, I re-read scriptures such as these that further enlightened me about such a powerful word, love: Romans 5:8; 1 Corinthians 13; Galatians 5:22, and Psalm 91:14. These are some of the books, chapters, and verses that confirmed God's motives for us.

People are the only created thing that God described as being made in His own image. This is a significant discovery. Since we are made in His image (free will, inventors, creators, and so forth), then everything that He created was created for us simply because He thinks so much of us. Love equals provision, and provision reciprocates.

As I continue this quest to find out who God is to me and me to Him, I begin examining the second commandment, which is to love my neighbor as myself. Since love has been defined in the previous text, it must now be put into action. So, what does it mean to love my neighbor as myself?

The first thing that must be qualified is whether I love myself. The truth is, I had not given much thought to loving myself until now. Now that I am thinking of that, I must say that I cannot love anyone as I am. My fallen nature will not allow me to do so because it is automatically selfish. It wants and does not give, and it takes without considering others.

The only way that I can demonstrate love is to be transformed into God's image, meaning, to adopt His nature. The only way to adopt Christ's nature is to battle with mine when a situation presents itself. The conclusion, thus, becomes denying myself for the sake of others. That's how I could love my neighbor as myself.

John 3:16 defines the epitome of love. In that verse, the sacrifice is clearly seen as God's ultimate gift of Himself by allowing His only begotten to be crucified so that others can live. From that example, the only way to love my neighbor is to demonstrate the same sacrifice, which is giving up myself in order to be of help.

I recall three separate instances that depict giving up my desires in consideration of someone else (an actual neighbor). I reside next door to an elderly person. Our driveway or parking spaces are close to each other. It's more convenient for me if I park my vehicle at a certain angle; however, it would inconvenience my neighbor, so I do not.

Additionally, though I enjoy listening to music, I am careful not disturb him, so I keep the volume at a level that will not. Also, when I sweep my driveway, I sweep his driveway as well, though he does not ask. These are simple acts of kindness that consider someone else over myself.

When a future circumstance presents itself to deny or consider someone else besides myself, I may have to do battle with my flesh nature, but if I am sincere about being transformed into the image of Christ, He will see me through.

It is therefore clear that God does not wave a magic wand and give me what I want. No. That is not His character. This journey is one that disciplines me. It's causing me to be held accountable and not blame others, especially God, for unsatisfactory conditions that I may encounter.

As stated before, I live in a society where buying and selling are essential. I have responsibilities to take care of, so it is necessary to have the means to do so honestly and responsibly. If I need a job to be able to take care of my responsibilities, I will not sit around, pout, and blame God for my bills not being paid.

The book of James 2:14-26 (KJV) clearly states that faith without works is dead. This means that I will have to literally make an effort to find a job that will provide the means to take care of my responsibilities. The scriptures clearly state that if we seek wisdom, God will grant it. This means that if I ask God to impart wisdom to me to find a specific job, He will grant it.

In the New Testament, He said, "Seek, and we will find; knock, and the door shall be opened. I have to take Him at His word and believe that He will honor it. I have come to realize that God is not complicated; mankind can be.

If I have a problem with losing weight, I am not going to ask the Lord to help me to lose weight. No. That is not how He functions. He is not my personal butler. To lose the weight, I would begin with how much food I was consuming and the kinds of food as well. Because I trained my body to practice such eating habits for so long, I would need to discipline myself to reverse it.

It would not be easy initially, but with much practice and determination, I would lose the weight. Such an approach would increase my faith to face any other challenges that I more than likely would encounter. This is the difference between being a slave and a son or a master and a Lord.

CHAPTER 37: RESTING IN SONSHIP

A son (or daughter) is disciplined by the Father for the purpose of transferring His identity to them. The Father is hard-working. He also wants His offspring to be like Him, so He allows them to go through circumstances that teach them how to work for what they desire. That is what faith is. A slave is whipped into subjection. His only job is to perform. He does not have an identity because he has been trained by legalism. That's the law. The law has governors and tutors, whereas faith has Lordship or Fatherhood.

I was a slave for over 4 decades. For most of my life, I put my body through hardship, thinking that my hard work would grant me access to heaven. I could not hear the voice of God except on rare occasions when I found myself in difficult situations. Being a slave relieved me of accountability. It was easier to blame someone else for my downfalls or mishaps. I was in bondage to the very religious system that I sacrificed for. Nothing that I did was good enough. I could not fast enough, pray enough, or keep up with the rituals. The more that I gave, the more I was asked to give. I was in great bondage that caused blindness and deafness to the Holy Spirit.

When I realized that my work not mixed with faith was not getting me anywhere, I knew that I was on the wrong foundation. Out of desperation, I cried out to the Lord. He heard my cry and sent deliverance from slavery. I am now a son (or daughter) with an identity in Christ Jesus.

Sonship (or daughter) is the most significant identity in Christ. It signifies access to the kingdom of God because of birthright or obedience to Jesus Christ. Birthright is not forced, manipulated, or achieved by one's own effort. This type of birthright is initiated by Jesus first, and the recipient chooses or refuses the offer.

When I realized that Jesus Christ granted me access, it was

difficult to receive because I thought that my works would be sufficient. Not so. Being granted access to His kingdom is not dependent on my efforts, only my obedience. I struggle with this truth even today.

For instance, when I find myself resting from my daily toils, I feel guilty. The guilt comes from the foundation of always finding something to do. I would convince myself that someone or something needs my attention, and I would even go seeking it out. I recall talking to my youngest daughter about her day at school. As I began talking with her, her response was, "Mom, I'm ok. There is nothing to worry about.

I had to gather myself and allow her response to resonate. After a slight pause, I said okay. At that moment, I realized that I did not have to worry about her. If she needed me, she knew that I would have been available for her. I had to then choose to believe what she said, or complicate matters for her. It was difficult for me to accept what she said, but I did not want to complicate things for her.

That is an example of many that I struggled with, even after the Lord granted access to His kingdom. At one point, I asked the Lord to forgive me for frustrating His grace. A special person once said to me, He (the Lord) was not in the wind; He was a still, small voice.

That statement reassured me that though God could have spoken through the wind, which represented force, He chose to speak in a gentle fashion, which represented calm strength. So it is with true salvation. It's not by power, nor by might, but by His Spirit. If I believe that this statement is true, then work/performance becomes obsolete.

Hebrews 4:9-10 (NIV) speaks of a sabbath rest for the people of God. With humility and confidence in Christ, I believe that I am experiencing such a rest. This rest is peaceful and assuring, yet volatile. Volatility is present because this rest is not like the natural where it's determined by resting after physically laboring. This rest is one that exists whether or not times are stable or not, but this rest is also determined by continued trust and dependency in Jesus.

Jesus declares in the scriptures that His kingdom is not of this world. I can attest to that saying because His kingdom is one that is built on truth, honesty, and integrity. It does not accept bribery, and it cannot be bought. There are no clicks, sects, or class systems. Everyone is equal in the King's presence, and the only exalted one is Jesus. That's why He reigns as King of kings and Lord of lords.

The reason why there is such a unique peace in the Kingdom of God is that there is proper order. When proper order exists, then the subjects are at peace. The Bible speaks of the order of God in such a way that when it's operating according to how God intended it to function, the people will be at peace. This order is found in 1 Corinthians 11:13: The head of Christ is God, the head of man is Christ, and the head of a woman is man (NLT). Here, it is clear that God Himself had provisions for mankind to be able to function decently and in order.

I am a firm believer in this order, so much so that I sacrificed to it for over 3 decades until God revealed to me that the order or authority was being abused.

God is a good Father. His inspired words that are outlined in the Bible are meant for good for those who embrace them. Sadly, sometimes they are used for selfish gain or selfish ambition, thus, abusing or violating the very essence of what the scriptures were intended to accomplish. When I witnessed that actually taking place, I was in complete denial. I did not want to accept that someone would deliberately violate the order of God without conviction.

Personally, I embrace lordship. As a matter of fact, it stems from my upbringing with my earthly father providing for me until I was almost 20 years old. Because of that foundation of being subjected to him, it was natural for that submission or allegiance to transfer to a husband or pastor. God did not intend for His divine order, which is depicted in the previous scriptures, to be used for selfish gain. When that happens, the subject will be misled and will go through great deception.

Because the order is divinely inspired, God will not allow such practice to continue, especially when the subordinate's trust is in God and not man. Psalm 138:2 (KJV) states that God magnifies His word above his name. I take courage, knowing that God is faithful to His word, but I must be careful to trust what the word of God says.

I spend most of my time asking the Lord for wisdom and understanding of how to implement His words in my life. Because the scripture clearly states that Man should not live by bread alone, but by every word that comes from the mouth of God (Matthew 4:4, KJV), it is imperative that I have an understanding of scripture. The Bible seems to contradict itself, so unless I have discernment of the scriptures, I will be in confusion.

Therefore, my quest is to continue seeking Him, the Bread of life, and allow His words to take root in my heart so that I can continue establishing a healthy relationship with Him. Selah.

Credits: https://biblehub.com

ABOUT THE AUTHOR

Winsome Patricia Marshall was born in Clarendon, Jamaica, to Earl Winston Marshall and Cecilia Johnson-Marshall. She migrated to the United States in the early 1990s, where she later met and married the father of her three daughters: Maria, Loretta, and Lauren. After dedicating several years as a stay-at-home mother and educator to her children, Winsome pursued a career in public education. She went on to earn a master's degree in education and currently serves at a Title I school.

Winsome's passion for writing grew out of her keen observation of life and her deep care for humanity. She is on a personal quest of self-discovery, with the hope of inspiring and guiding others along their own journeys. As she has expressed, "There must be more to life than just about me." With a heart that cannot rest until it finds answers to life's purpose, Winsome views *The Journey Within* as one meaningful step toward that greater calling.